European Cross-Sections

Compilation of pictures by Manfred Schütz

Text by Reiner Frenzel

PALACES
OF EUROPE

HART PUBLISHING COMPANY, INC.

NEW YORK CITY

TYPOGRAPHY AND DESIGN BY WALTER SCHILLER
COPYRIGHT 1970 BY EDITION LEIPZIG
FIRST AMERICAN PUBLICATION 1972
LIBRARY OF CONGRESS CATALOG NO. 79-186670
SBN NO. 8055-1030-3
PRINTED IN THE GERMAN DEMOCRATIC REPUBLIC

If a group of sight-seeing enthusiasts are asked whether they would rather be shown around an old city, a beautiful town hall, a church of historic and architectural interest or a princely residence, we can be reasonably certain that the latter will be their first choice.

Nowadays, when castles and palaces have long ceased to serve their original purpose, even though in some places they may still be the domicile of the surviving representatives of an *ancien régime*, what is it that attracts all sorts of people so strongly to the great Renaissance and Baroque houses throughout the countries of Europe? – The fact, perhaps, that something has been thrown open to them and may be freely visited, which up till now has been inaccessible to people of their class. They can roam around what was once the regional seat of authority and find no doors – or hardly any – closed to them. The interest in the history, whether of important events or of people who were involved in them, is sometimes combined with an almost childish curiosity. But an invariable adjunct is delight in the beautiful things with which the high and mighty extravagantly surrounded themselves, firstly because those things served to emphasize their rank and station, and secondly because of the entertainment and pleasure they gave, so providing what to some is the highest life can offer.

This also indicates the kind of conditions that gave rise to buildings such as palaces and castles, namely the division of human society into rich and poor, into rulers and oppressed. In prehistoric times there were no palaces, but only cave-dwellings or huts, none of which stood out by its size and grandeur or exceeded the measure of immediate human requirements.

The first luxurious buildings came into being when, towards the end of the fourth and the beginning of the third millennium BC, in the more highly developed civilizations of Mesopotamia, the Nile Valley and Crete, the primal human community began to break up because the accumulation of personal possessions favored the rise of an aristocratic ruling class in a tribal society. This class provided priests, tribal leaders and kings who, in many ancient cultures, were soon accorded divine honors. This combination of secular and religious power gave rise to the palace, containing both the ruler's apartments and the temple. A splendid example of this is the palace of the mythical king Minos at Knossos in Crete, excavated by Arthur Evans in 1899. The palace of the Cretan king is the archetype of the Minotaur's "labyrinth" in Greek mythology. Both the name, which means "house of the double axe," and the stylized bull's horns, which are the chief ornament on the buildings, show that the palace was intimately connected with the Cretan cult

Reconstruction of the palace at Knossos

of the bull. Besides the king's private rooms, the palace contained the throne room and innumerable domestic quarters and magazines, as well as places of worship and ceremonial roads. The vast flights of steps were used for religious pageantry and thus can be seen as early forerunners of the Greek theatre of classical times.

What has been preserved of the frescos dating from different building periods testifies to an astonishing mastery of color and artistic technique. Unlike the palaces of Egypt and the Near East, Knossos probably never had any defensive structures.

The palace was finally destroyed about 1400 BC. Some parts of the building that can be seen today were rebuilt after the excavations.

Fortified palaces, and the new towns that grew up immediately around them, paved the way both in the Peloponnese and on the Greek mainland for what was to be during the next two millennia the prevailing type of fortified dwelling, the castle. The palace building which had already reached such a splendid degree of development, no longer served any purpose in Ancient Greece after the occupation of this region by the Dorians whose social stratification was much more primitive, merely possessing a military leading caste, but no privileged rulers. In the Greek city-states of the centuries that followed, especially in the era of democracy, there was no need for great palaces. Thus later on in Europe, when the changed structure of human society once again demanded a style of architecture that would reflect the status of the ruling class, it became necessary to evolve a new form that would answer the requirements of a palace. But the Greek architectonic tradition was to persist without interruption.

Except in late Antiquity, the Italy of ancient times, which was partially colonized

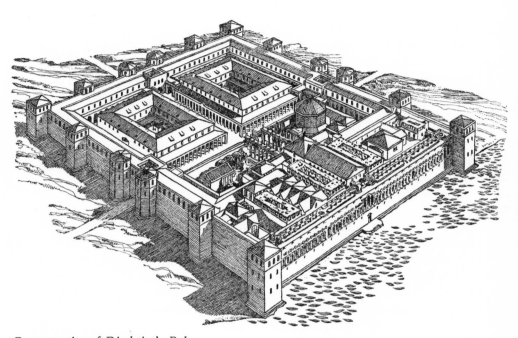

Reconstruction of Diocletian's Palace

by Greeks but where indigenous elements of Italo-Etruscan origin also continued to survive, possessed no palatial structures such as those in Mesopotamia or Crete. When in town, Roman aristocrats liked to live, after the Greek pattern, in an atrium house; but when they visited their big estates outside the city walls, they lived in villas.

It was not until the time of the Caesars that we once more encountered buildings whose luxury and size were intended to reflect the greatness and power of their owners: Nero's "Golden House", for example, or Hadrian's Villa in Tivoli. The first structure to meet all the requirements of a palace was the Flavian palace on the Palatine in Rome. Around one of the two inner courtyards were built all the rooms of state, such as the audience chamber, the judgement room, the banqueting hall and the private temple; round the other, the private apartments with their valuable furnishings for the emperor and his family.

6

Practically nothing of all this remains; what we know comes from the literature of the time or from excavations.

There was, however, another Roman building tradition which was to be of the utmost significance in European castle architecture: the fortified military camp, the *castrum*. In all their colonies, in Africa as in Gaul or in the Danube basin, the Romans built these fortifications, always with the same regular layout. Two streets intersecting at right angles formed the North–South and East–West axes of the rectangular site. Each of the four gates in the walls was fortified by the addition of towers, as were the four corners. Up till the time of the Renaissance, fortifications continued to be built on this pattern.

A fine palace constructed on these principles at Spalato (now Split, on the Adriatic coast of Yugoslavia) was built around AD 300 by the Emperor Diocletian as a residence for his old age. In the four quarters formed by the intersecting streets are the temple, the mausoleum, the women's quarters and the officials' quarters. With the partition of the West Roman Empire, imperial residences, or *palatia*, were built in the new capitals; these houses also contained the administrative offices.

This imperial style of architecture in late Antiquity led on to that of the Frankish kings whose palaces were not, however, built in a capital city but in numerous places throughout the Empire, serving as residences for the king and his entire retinue as he travelled about his dominions. The vexed question of whether or not these ancient palaces were fortified is of little more interest than the question of their direct association with the royal estates which ensured supplies for the numerous retainers. But these edifices must necessarily have possessed a hall for imperial assemblies, a chapel and royal apartments. During the Carolingian and Ottonian periods, the extent and importance of these palaces varied with the preferences of individual emperors and kings so that now one, now the other would assume almost the character of a permanent residence. Such, in Germany, were Aachen, Quedlinburg and Goslar. By a stroke of good fortune, Charles the Great's lovely chapel has survived at Aachen; nothing remains of these palatine residences but ruins. But we know that at least some were equipped with the comforts possessed by the buildings of Antiquity, such as under-floor heating.

Besides palatine residences, there were also imperial castles, essential for the protection of the ruler in those turbulent times, and throughout the Middle Ages we find a huge number of castles belonging to the greater and lesser nobility. The site and

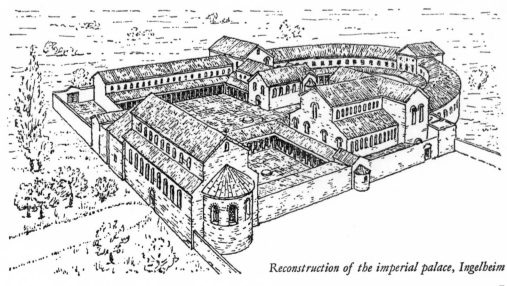

Reconstruction of the imperial palace, Ingelheim

nature of the castle was determined by the requirements of defense. Thus the construction was adapted to the chosen site and the appearance of the castle was determined by the natural features of the landscape. Favorable positions were on a hilltop, or at the end of a ridge with easily defended approaches, or again on an island in a river or lake, not too far from the bank.

Even where the terrain did not favor the building of a castle, natural features were adapted to the requirements of defense and deep moats were dug, or barbicans were built. Where the terrain did not determine the design of the castle we usually find the rectangular keep. Domestic comfort was invariably sacrificed to strong fortifications. Life was somewhat pleasanter however in the hereditary castles of the more powerful princely families. These

castles were often situated in the heart of the ruler's domains and were thus protected by other castles. Here were assembled the lesser feoffees and the "flower of the Middle Ages" – the knights. Such castles were residences and centers of social life, and were furnished with corresponding splendor.

In the late Middle Ages the secular buildings most akin to later château architecture in their artistic embellishments as well as in their attempts to provide domestic comfort, are those of the Hohenstaufen emperor, Frederick II. Most of those erected in Italy at his orders are still, from the outside, fortifications or keeps, but they contain great halls with columns and vaulted ceilings designed to enhance the imperial renown. Of these the most individual as well as the most significant in the development of castle architec-

ture is the Castel del Monte in Apulia which was built as a hunting castle in the middle of an almost uninhabited tract of country. Even the exterior is unusual, being a regular octagon with octagonal turrets at each angle. The red entrance gate set in golden-brown rusticated masonry enhances the monumental effect of the building which stands on its own, encircling the top of the hill like a crown. In commissioning buildings Frederick II gave express orders to his favorite architect, Richard of Lentini, that he should also aim at convenience and domestic comfort.

These wishes were realized in the interior of Castel del Monte, too, although from the outside it still seemed stern and inhospitable. This was achieved in a way that was quite new in the thirteenth century, for in the towers which also served to carry staircases to the upper floors, there were bedrooms with adjoining bath, magnificent chimney pieces and even flushing water-closets. The throne room lay above the entrance gate. Originally all the rooms on the upper floor were connected by a wooden gallery. It is difficult to say with certainty whether these astonishing interior arrangements were the result of a conscious reversion to the domestic architecture of Antiquity, or whether they heralded the new outlook of the then imminent Renaissance which was itself to draw so largely on classical sources.

Hohenstaufen castle Castel del Monte

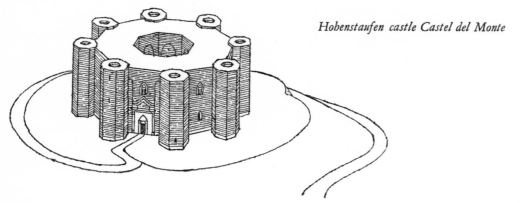

During the crusades a great many feudal lords and knights became acquainted with the more refined way of life of the Saracenic rulers and of the Christian descendants of the East Roman Empire in Constantinople, a city which the alleged "defenders of Christendom" had, in most unchristian fashion, conquered, ravaged and pillaged in 1204. Again, increased trade with the Levant brought quantities of oriental luxury goods to Europe. The newly acquired knowledge of Saracenic fortification resulted in a spate of castle building in Europe at the end of the thirteenth century, but everywhere there were signs of a demand for domestic comfort. In Italy, however, new social forces were at work which were to bring about a complete change in domestic architecture. After the death of the Hohenstaufen emperor Frederick II, Italy's foreign overlord, the power of the Holy Roman Empire under German rule collapsed. Politics during the three centuries that followed were dominated by five increasingly powerful states – Florence, Milan, Venice, Naples together with Sicily, and the Papal States. Each of the five sought in vain to unite the whole of Italy under its own rule. The holders of power were no longer the hereditary nobility who were, indeed, now partially excluded by law from taking a direct part in governing. In Milan, Venice and Florence, city-states grown rich through foreign trade and manufacture, power was in the hands of the upper middle classes, but not without opposition from the lower middle classes. Naples remained a pawn in the game of foreign powers; it passed from the hands of French kings of the houses of Anjou and Valois into those of their Spanish rivals, the house of Aragon.

The new rulers in the city-states of the fourteenth and fifteenth centuries were merchant bankers with immense and far-reaching connections, such as the Medici in Florence, or else successful condottieri such as the Montefeltro in Urbino and the Gonzaga in Mantua. They lived in the cities, but so long as the question of supremacy remained undecided and blood continued to flow in the struggles between rival families or classes, their palaces outwardly retained the appearance of a stronghold and were protected by powerful rusticated masonry. Within, however, a gentler architecture prevailed in courtyards and rooms. A delight in ornament and the urge for artistic perfection in every detail and every part of the building eliminated the difference between civic and private secular architecture on the one hand and church architecture on the other, which throughout Europe during the Middle Ages had taken pride of place. In the Italian Renaissance the splendid churches as well as the palaces were built by the same artists, who also produced the sculptures and paintings for their decoration – Brunelleschi, for instance, or Michelozzo, Sangallo, Raphael, Bramante, Mantegna or Sansovino. These great masters of Italian art not only served the new ruling class but generally belonged to the intimate circle of the great and were, moreover, well aware of their own value. For them, national frontiers meant little. Their works were known and appreciated by the princes of other countries, and they were invited to undertake the building or rebuilding of royal and princely residences which were designed to impress.

Meanwhile in other countries there had been a more or less marked shift in economic dependency. With the development of a money economy, which superseded the simple exchange of consumer goods, the town became the chief economic center. Influential nobles were anxious to come to terms financially with the newly rich burghers, but more often than not became dependent on the great merchant bankers as a result of their constant borrowing.

The lesser nobility had their own way of sharing in the new prosperity. With their armed bands they would fall upon trade caravans, seizing money and goods and often extorting ransom. The castles of the lesser nobility became the lairs of robber knights, provoking the hatred of the despoiled merchants and their cities.

Another reason for the dwindling importance of the castles was the development of ordnance which soon came to be generally used in warfare. Castles, like the feudalism of the Middle Ages, had become outdated, and their place was taken by a new kind of feudal residence. Their defensive function could only be assumed by strongholds designed to resist ordnance, a function which was soon to become divorced from domestic architecture.

The heyday of château architecture in France began in the fifteenth century when the king had succeeded in centralizing his power, so that in essentials the country assumed the form it still retains today. During the reign of Francis I, the building of Chambord and Fontainebleau produced the first great French Renaissance châteaux, and the Château de Blois, which had already been added to under his predecessor Louis XII, received an extension in the form of a finely proportioned wing with a magnificent projecting staircase tower. Blois and Fontainebleau, in accordance with late medieval custom, still consisted of an apparently random cluster of individual buildings, whereas Chambord was a building of unified style. Many people have sought to associate the design of this symmetrical building with Leonardo da Vinci, who died in 1519 at Amboise, not far from Chambord. There is no conclusive proof of this, but the château undoubtedly derives from the Italian *castello*. The influence of Italian architecture which is everywhere apparent was indirectly disseminated by the books of the great Italian architectural authorities which were studied throughout Europe, but it was also transmitted directly.

Louis XII had been sent a model in wood for a castle, at his own request, by Pope Julius II, and Francis I continually tried to attract great Italian artists to his court. In 1546 Michelangelo himself received a tempting invitation, but having already ignored repeated personal requests from the Pope to return to Rome, he politely refused the French king's offer.

Buildings such as Chambord set the standard for Renaissance architecture north of the Alps – a symmetrical ensemble with a ground plan that was purely geometrical. The desire for variety could find expression in anything from simple forms, the rectangle or circle, to the most complex polygonal and star shapes, such as are found in the Château de Maune (France) or later in Kryztopor in Poland, or again in the Castle of Hvězda (star) near Prague. Now it was no longer the terrain, but a grasp of mathematics, resulting from the progress made in the new natural sciences, which determined the form of the individual building and which induced a growing preoccupation with the unified planning of whole cities.

This predilection found particular expression in the layout of gardens which were regarded as an essential adjunct to the residences of the wealthy classes. From modest beginnings in the small medieval monastery or castle garden, familiar to us mainly from miniatures and woodcuts, places of meditation and courtly wooing, where the vegetation was natural and informal – there developed in the Renaissance the great gardens consisting of an ornamental arrangement of strictly symmetrical areas. The position of every flower looks as though it had been planned with rule and compass – as, indeed, it has – and no twig is allowed to trespass outside the shape which has been laid down for tree or bush. As yet, the garden was still used in much the same way as before. By degrees, however, the quiet retreat was to be invaded by festive gatherings, big, noisy and informal.

In Renaissance and, later on, Baroque books and pictures, the garden is no longer depicted as the haunt of dreamy lovers, but as the scene of frankly erotic delights, enjoyed by a society freed from its medieval religious restraints. In grounds, ever more extensive, water was put to many uses – artificial rivers, still lakes, or the treacherous trick fountain, springing up and disappearing suddenly to surprise the unwary and sprinkle them with its benison on paths, seats, or beneath artificial trees. A late example of this kind, which was

A castle of the fortified type –
St. Johannisburg, Aschaffenburg

once so popular in Germany, is found in the park of Peterhof near Leningrad; tourists find it amusing, if at times somewhat damping. But having explored this idiosyncratic byway, we must now return to architecture proper.

By comparison with the narrow stair turrets of medieval times, a significant innovation in building design was the spiral staircase, finely constructed, splendidly decorated, and of increasingly generous proportions. North of the Alps this was the forerunner of the right-angled staircase. At Blois, in the Albrechtsburg at Meissen and at neighboring Torgau, the staircase towers still project as in medieval times, from the outside wall, but at Chambord a double spiral staircase inside the building rises from floor to floor.

The Albrechtsburg in Meissen is worthy of special note. Anyone who has ever browsed through one of the countless books on castles and palaces, or has listened attentively to a castellan reverently holding forth on the history of his castle, knows that the majority of these buildings have arisen on the site or the foundations of an earlier structure. One of the reasons for this is the major part played by tradition in noble families, but there have also been practical considerations. Again the number of castles in Europe is estimated at between one hundred and two hundred thousand, but this is probably on the low side, and having regard to their random distribution over the countryside, later generations in search of a site for a stately home, both convenient for communications and set in pleasing surroundings, could hardly have failed to stumble on the foundations, at least, of an earlier structure.

In the case of Albrechtsburg, the castle – or rather, residence – for the Duke of Saxony and his brother was built on a hill above the town of Meissen about 1470, just at the time when the building of châteaux was taking the place of fortified castles. Thus Albrechtsburg is perhaps the clearest example in Europe of the transition from a traditional castle, which it resembles both in its position and its outward appearance, to a princely residence with large, vaulted halls and tall, late Gothic windows facing onto the courtyard. Almost simultaneously the Vladislav Hall was built in a related style on the Hradčany in Prague. Signs of transition are more frequently to be found in the moated, riparian or island castles in the plains, of which examples could be given in nearly every European country; here we shall only mention Gripsholm in Sweden.

The social upheavals which, in many countries of Europe, led to the Reformation, though they reduced the power of the Catholic Church did not bring about any discernible alienation from Christianity. Religion retained its importance in a society that was moving towards absolutism; indeed, in Catholic areas, nobility and clergy were more strongly allied during the Counter-Reformation than they had ever been before. Hence the chapel remained an integral part of palace precincts, whether the court was Catholic or Protestant.

So far as the visual arts were concerned, however, the Renaissance meant the end of the predominance of Church patronage which had so largely dictated the subject matter. With the new value accorded to art, the collection of *objets d'art* received considerable impetus and in princely residences, rooms were set aside for curios and works of art. Probably the finest example of this is the *Antiquarium* in the Residenz at Munich, which is a gallery for classical portrait busts. After 1580 the Austrian Archduke Ferdinand II had five rooms added to Schloss Ambras to house his valuable collection of weapons and works of art; it was the first large building of its kind. Thus, as time went on separate buildings adapted to all the functions proper to a princely court were added to the original residence. Utilitarian buildings, such as stables, formerly accorded only secondary importance, were now enlarged and given a form in keeping with the love felt for the noble steeds they contained. Even the name underwent a change; *Marstall* was considered a more fitting appellation. The desire for ostentation exemplified in choice entertainments and festivities gave rise to the *Lustschloss* – a term ambiguous to modern ears and perhaps not without reason in view of the frequently dissipated life led by the aristocracy in the seventeenth century. This architectural assignment – a château in its own park, usually outside the city walls, solely designed for pleasure and festivity and wholly distinct from the town residence with its social and administrative duties – is linked with a new type of building, the single block containing one large hall with ancillary rooms. The best surviving example of this is the Belvedere in Prague, in the immediate vicinity of the Hradčany. Large houses specially designed as hunting lodges were built in the vast forests where formerly there had been common rights but where the feudal lords had now asserted their exclusive claim, which they safeguarded with severe penalties. In this way there gradually arose a series of feudal domestic buildings for permanent or seasonal residence, their diversity depending not only on the owner's social position or his personal tastes, but also on the *Zeitgeist*.

The building of these great houses encouraged not architecture alone, but interior decoration as well, and hence the production of artistically valuable tapestries and hangings, furniture and mosaic floors. The men responsible for carrying out all the work involved in these schemes were no longer anonymous like the artists and craftsmen of the Middle Ages. We know the names of nearly all the architects, painters, stuccoworkers and landscape gardeners. From account books and building records we even know those of the masons and laborers.

After the sixteenth century the names of architects and decorators indicated in these documents are often Italian or Dutch. During their travels in Italy a great many noblemen engaged the pupils of great Italian artists for work on their palaces. This was true of Spain, as of France, Germany or Poland; Italian builders even penetrated to Moscow.

Holland set the standard for the decorative architectural features that attained such popularity north of the Alps. While Dutch decorative engravers such as Cornelis Floris and Vredeman de Vries did, of course, exert a direct influence, their work became widely known through the dissemination of their engravings and through their pupils, and is evident in urban architecture as well as in the château architecture of Germany, Poland, Denmark and Sweden. Dutch influence manifests

itself, not only in the decoration of interiors and exteriors, but also in colored ornamental brickwork. Red brick walls patterned with light-colored sandstone are always evidence of Dutch influence. Yet by comparing these with other buildings in the same area it may be seen how foreign traditions blend with native characteristics to form an idiosyncratic style in keeping both with the period and the landscape.

At the same time new artistic currents were evolving in Italy as a result of the Counter Reformation's intensified religious propaganda after the conclusion of the Council of Trent in 1563. The tasks assigned to religious painting and music were uncompromising and binding; in architecture the effects were unmistakable. The basic principle was no longer well-balanced proportion and a logical construction, but the use of variation in spatial effect and the internal and external dynamics of architectural features, as well as an overstatement of individual forms to appeal to the sensibilities of the beholder and to influence his emotions.

Church architecture experienced a new flowering, both inside Italy and elsewhere in Catholic areas. The building of churches and great houses was influenced in both cases by the desire to express grandeur and power. During the Renaissance, painting and sculpture had become associated with architecture, but now all the artistic media

were combined, and even music, drama and ceremonial were used to enhance the total effect of the building. Façades were given plasticity and depth by boldly projecting or recessed architectural features, by pediments and huge colonnades. Within, frescos and plaster decorations gave an illusory sense of space, painted architecture merged imperceptibly into three-dimensional architecture, and painted figures were often given plaster limbs.

There is no other stylistic epoch that has striven so much for outer effect as the Baroque. Absolutism was the social soil from which it sprang. In France especially, the monarchy, aided by the growing strength of the bourgeoisie, had gathered all the power into its own hands after subjugating the nobility who had opposed a unified state. They now became parasites at the court of monarchs who, for their part, did what they could to prevent the rise of a civic state. The same thing was happening in Spain, which was, however, finally to lose her position as a great power in the eighteenth century. Germany and Italy, however, came under the rule of innumerable petty despots who, by the architecture of their residences and the magnificence of their courts, sought to ape the French king in a display of power most of them did not possess. Only in England and Holland did the economically entrenched merchants succeed in assuming political power and restricting the status of the monarchy. In Russia at this time the Middle Ages were only just drawing to a close. Thus Europe presented a whole range of different social conditions which were directly reflected in secular architecture.

The leading role was played by the French monarchy, by Louis XIV whose Palace of Versailles outside the gates of Paris became the incontestable prototype for the great Baroque residences in Europe. There were two reasons for its position immediately outside the capital: firstly, the lack of space inside the city where such a vast site could only have been accommodated by razing whole quarters and secondly – and this was the main incentive – the desire to be set apart from the "common people", the desire for exclusivity. In building Versailles, Louis XIV was in turn influenced by the Château de Vaux-le-Vicomte which Fouquet, the Superintendent of Finance, had had built with money obviously obtained by the misappropriation of taxes. During the inaugural festivities, the colossal scale of Fouquet's ambitions as well as contemporary ideas on the interplay of all the different kinds of art were revealed. In the presence of the youthful king, Molière performed one of his comedies and La Fontaine read a poem praising the amazing transformation that had been effected. Not long after this the owner of the château was arrested, dismissed from office and

deprived of all the property he had so unlawfully gained.

To build Versailles, Louis XIV engaged the services of the masters who had been responsible for Vaux-le-Vicomte – the architect Le Vau, the landscape gardener Le Nôtre and the interior designer Le Brun. If to these we add the name of Jules Hardouin-Mansart, the list of those mainly responsible for French château architecture in the seventeenth century is complete. The creations of these artists, and indeed of French art generally, diverged from the exuberance of Baroque forms, and were altogether more reserved and sedate while still retaining their pathos. The same is true of England whose architecture, with few exceptions, followed in the footsteps of the Italian Renaissance architect, Andrea Palladio. His buildings, especially the Villa Rotonda, were characterized by the traditional classical forms and they exerted a tremendous influence on English and Dutch artists long before 1770 which was about the time when the classical revival began to borrow so largely from the art and culture of Antiquity. These three tendencies – the French classical, the classical Palladian, and the exuberance of Italian Baroque – are variously found in the château architecture of Germany, Russia, Sweden and the countries under Habsburg rule – that is, Austria, Hungary and Bohemia. In and around Vienna after 1700 there

arose great houses such as Schönbrunn and Belvedere, designed by J. Bernhard Fischer von Erlach and Lukas von Hildebrandt.

At the same time the capital cities of Prussia and Sweden saw the growth of huge residences. In 1708 Peter the Great transferred the Russian capital from Moscow to his newly founded city of St. Petersburg, where he ordered the building of large residences including the great palace of Peterhof. Besides the large groups of buildings erected by absolutist monarchs, there were also the many palatial mansions and country seats of the aristocracy grown rich in the service of the state, and of petty despots, both ecclesiastical and secular. By his military and diplomatic prowess, Prince Eugene of Savoy, whom Louis XIV so much despised, was able to achieve an almost impregnable position in Austria as his residences, both there and in Hungary, testify. His friend, the Duke of Marlborough – Churchill's ancestor – and, like Eugene, a soldier and royal adviser, was less fortunate; disgraced, he went into voluntary exile, leaving the completion of his palace in his wife's hands. Cardinal Wolsey, though he had to cede his palace to his king's envy, succeeded in retaining his liberty – unlike men such as Fouquet whose disgrace, imprisonment or exile left their estates – and especially their houses – to fall like ripe fruit into the laps of their liege-lords.

The majority of the less influential aristocracy, however, had to content themselves with a town mansion with an exterior reminiscent of Italian Renaissance palaces. Prague, Vienna, Leningrad, Warsaw, Berlin and Dresden at one time contained great numbers of these houses belonging to the aristocracy, who lived a parasitical life at the imperial and royal courts. In France these houses were given the name of *hôtel*.

While they were in attendance at court, the courtiers lived in the lesser wings of the palace, the *corps de logis* on either side of the *cour d'honneur*. Under the French absolute monarchy, in particular, court ceremony and social pretensions dictated the organization of the building. The rooms were no longer regarded as having equal value, and whether a visitor was allowed to enter a particular room depended on his rank and the honor it was wished to accord him. The highest honor at the court of Louis XIV, the "Sun King", who proclaimed himself to be the embodiment of the state, was permission to attend the ceremonial *lever* and *coucher* in the royal bedchamber. Quite logically then, the bedchamber at Versailles occupied the central position normally reserved for the great staircase or for banqueting and reception rooms. Thus the most important room in the whole country was not the universally famous *Galerie des Glaces*, but the bedchamber of the Sun King. In the case of

his successor, Louis XV, the "well loved" (although it was really he who did the loving and who, even by comparison with his far from prudish predecessors, exceeded all bounds in his amorous pursuit of the young beauties of the land), such a reversal of values might have been understandable. But in fact he built the "deer park", his seraglio not far from the palace, where a succession of concubines was ensured by the diligence of a whole army of *procureurs* and women of dubious reputation.

Both the arrangement of rooms and the rich interiors were carefully calculated to impress the visitor. Instead of the ingenious stairway of earlier times there was an imposing staircase leading to a suite of rooms

which prepared the visitor for his meeting with the master of the house. The rooms were no longer connected by means of simple corridors; the visitor had to pass through each splendid room in order to reach the next and even more splendid one, until he finished up in the audience chamber. In the domestic architecture of the Renaissance, the secondary buildings had already been arranged in order of precedence around the main complex. Now all these buildings and those fulfilling new functions, such as theatre or opera, the attributes of the château, were mostly arranged symmetrically in the form of a horseshoe around the *cour d'honneur*, in progressively diminishing height, and, together with the gigantic

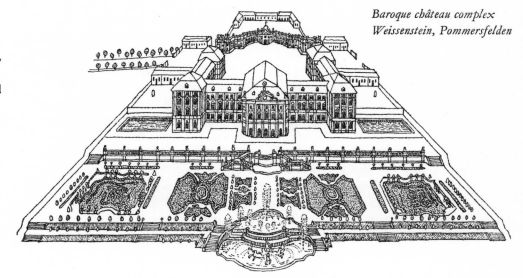

Baroque château complex Weissenstein, Pommersfelden

parks in which they stood, were planned and carried out as a unified whole to a much greater extent than had been done during the Renaissance. The plans would even include the neighboring village which usually housed the servants.

Great avenues converged symmetrically on the château and the same axial pattern was reproduced in the gardens by the use of a main avenue or a strip of water, or perhaps, as at Caserta, a system of cascades, extending over several miles. The park was no longer enclosed within walls but, as in the landscapes of the French painters Lorrain and Poussin, melted into a distant haze.

These excesses presage the end of vainglorious château building. The urge to ape great prototypes and to outdo one's neighbors, combined with the extremism inherent in Baroque, gave rise to completely impracticable plans, far in excess of available financial and material resources. Thus we often find, besides projects that had to be abandoned, the substitution of fake architecture for otherwise too expensive buildings. Another aspect of this was the imitation of costly materials, though this practice was by no means always confined to petty imitators of the great, for in the contemporary view the successful reproduction of more costly material was regarded as a positive achievement.

C. Northcote Parkinson, the great debunker, is not wholly wrong when in his *Parkinson's Law*, under the heading "Plans and Plants", he seeks to prove that great palaces often arise only when the power of those who build them is already in decline. He demonstrates this with the examples of Versailles, Buckingham Palace and Blenheim Palace. The accuracy of his assertion is also evident if applied to Stockholm. When the building of the new palace began, the dream of Sweden as a great power had already begun to vanish.

The building of châteaux in the post-Baroque era evolved in close association with the ideas of the Enlightenment. The enthusiasm for nature inspired by Rousseau was combined with a love of luxury, with pleasure-seeking and frivolous loose living typical of an effete society. The aim was no longer to impress; the demand now was for every comfort, in the company of like-minded friends. The true criterion of Rococo architecture is not the use of the shell motif, but harmony of interior decoration and furnishings, and its most valuable legacy is a previously unimaginable domestic culture. Hence the monarchy's and nobility's passion for building seldom expressed itself in the official city palace or mansion, but rather in the small, intimate country house, wholly free of urban ostentatiousness, where the owner could pursue his own inclinations. With very few exceptions, these châteaux did not conform to the Baroque plan of main block and two wings, but were closer to the Renaissance "pleasure house". Generally they took the form of a small wingless building having an oval-shaped main room at the center; most of the rooms had large French windows opening onto the garden or park.

After about 1750 the prevailing fashion was for what was styled "English" (as opposed to "French") gardens, in which the trees and bushes were planted in natural-looking clumps. Their popularity had been materially enhanced by Rousseau's passion for nature, and his theory that nature should remain unsullied by the works of man. In newly landscaped gardens there were many small buildings of symbolic nature, such as Greek temples, Egyptian pyramids, and artificial ruins which were supposed to testify to the victory of natural forces over the works of man.

There were countless châteaux in the second half of the eighteenth century that bore names such as "Hermitary", "Hermitage" or "Mon Plaisir". The inscription "Sans Souci" on the little château in Potsdam Park is a symbol of the times. The "back to nature" movement was even responsible for the building of a farm in the park at Versailles, the *Maison de la Reine*, where Marie-Antoinette used to retire to a pseudo-rural life in order to recover from her exhausting round of pleasures until in 1793 the guillotine put an end to her intrigues against the Revolution.

Even as early as the mid-eighteenth century, the French writer, Saint-Simon, was indirectly attacking the absolutist outlook with his sardonic criticism of the grounds of Versailles in his descriptions of life at the court of Louis XIV. The Voltairian ideal of an enlightened monarchy seemed an acceptable solution to the more far-seeing European monarchs such as Frederick the Great of Prussia and Russia's Catherine the Great, who were both personally acquainted with the philosopher. It was, they thought, a middle way between absolutism and revolution. Some of them may have realized that the times were moving towards *égalité*, and that too obvious a display of absolutism would endanger their own efforts to maintain their supremacy.

Thus the return to the villa architecture of Antiquity which, in Italy, had never completely disappeared, is probably indicative of a democratic frame of mind, though one that was seldom due to any genuine conviction. The main impetus here was the general preoccupation throughout Europe with the art and intellectual life of Antiquity, a preoccupation that was to lead to the efflorescence of the classical revival, the movement known as Classicism. An important part was played in this connection by the then recent excavations at Pompeii whose frescos exerted considerable influence upon interior decoration. There was a rage for Pompeian red, figurative scenes, and ornaments after the Pompeian model.

New houses and palaces with genuine classical forms were in fact rare; those in Kačina, Wörlitz, Pavlovsk near Leningrad and in the Lazienki Park in Warsaw are some of the few. Another is at Athens below the Acropolis, where the Munich court architect, Friedrich Gärtner, built a wide-fronted palace according to plans drawn up by his teacher, Leo von Klenze, for the newly invested Greek king, Otto, of the Bavarian house of Wittelsbach.

Otto was by no means king "by divine right", but had been placed on the throne in 1833 by the powers which had driven the Turks out of Greece. As the representative of those powers' interests, he had been given guarantees of security and a loan of sixty million francs. Friedrich Schinkel, the great Berlin Classicist, had previously drawn up plans for a château immediately behind the Parthenon as well as for an imperial residence in the Crimea which were to combine the outmoded architectural function of display with the newly-acquired classical forms. But his grandiose schemes never got further than the drawing-board, and only small châteaux near Berlin and in Lusatia were built from his designs. The heyday of château architecture came to an end with the victory of the bourgeoisie over absolutism.

A house of the villa type – Charlottenhof, Potsdam

The emphasis in architecture now shifted to civic and commercial building. Town halls, exchanges, post offices and stations, as well as industrial buildings were the new assignments, to which must be added the ostentatious villas of industrialists who wished to flaunt their newly acquired wealth. In big cities, there were theatres and museums to be built.

Those monarchs who still played a part in government could now choose between adapting some of the rooms in the palaces they had inherited to accord with the needs of the times, or building new, utilitarian residences using modern techniques and forms. A few of the more romantic reverted to medieval building forms in an endeavor to turn their backs on the progress made by human society and, from the towers of their newly built fake castles, to play once again at being powerful and influential liege-lords like their forefathers. As representatives of an effete society, they had no choice but to seek salvation in the past by selecting outmoded and even artistically sterile architectural and stylistic forms, for neither the present nor the future of their countries was in their hands.

An especially ignoble part was played in this respect by the insignificant German princelings who were ready at hand whenever a country seemed to require a royal figurehead, though the proffered crowns were in fact devoid of all influence. For the destiny of the principalities was no longer decided in princely residences, but in parliamentary buildings.

The town and country mansions of the nobility, insofar as their owners' financial position could run to modernization, continued to fulfil their domestic role – as indeed, some of them still do today, except in places where the social structure has undergone revolutionary changes which have deprived the lord of his manor. In some countries of Europe the "upper ten thousand" still use as a status symbol the great houses they have inherited or bought. They provide the newly-rich snobs, the celebrities and industrialists, with a historical background – proof of their own importance – and with an exclusive setting for their social entertainment, just as they used to do for the aristocracy. To anyone with any feeling for the needs of our era, it can only seem a living anachronism that in Austria, where the nobility was abolished in 1919, Prince Esterházy should go on trying to keep up appearances at his castle of Eisenstadt.

But what was to be done with buildings which no longer served their original purpose? An important new function was presaged as early as 1793, when, during the French Revolution, the Convention nationalized the royal art treasures and put them on public display in the Louvre. At that time, too, Gustav III of Sweden had some of the rooms at the palace in Stockholm converted into a public art gallery. Since then great houses and palaces in many places have been put to such use. In Leningrad the Winter Palace became the home of the famous Hermitage collections. In Bucharest, Rome, Florence, Munich and elsewhere, works of art were also accommodated in great houses and palaces.

Historic houses of artistic and cultural interest were also thrown open for public conducted tours so that every year millions of visitors are able to obtain a true idea of the life and culture of the former occupants and of the times when the buildings arose, which in turn permits them to appreciate the skill of the artists responsible. But the nature and quality of these tours varies considerably, for they range from the tape-recorded lecture in several languages which rattles away at the bands of visitors following close on each other's heels, to the sedate, official caretaker who, in return for a tip, will relate the chief events in his former master's family history. Then there is the attractive young female guide whose eyes twinkle mischievously during her lecture in the state bedroom, thus reducing to a minimum the attention of her male listeners who are busily engaged in imagining themselves to be the *seigneur* himself.

Again, some of these houses now also serve to put people up, whether they are convalescents, schoolchildren, newly-weds or impecunious men of letters. There are a great many holiday homes in what used to be mansions and castles. More than two hundred have been converted into hotels and restaurants. In most cases this required considerable rebuilding, for nowadays we are a good deal more particular about amenities and domestic comfort than were the people of the seventeenth and eighteenth centuries. For who, today, would want to spend a holiday in a hotel room without a bath, or one without any sort of heating? True, there was a bath in Versailles in Louis XIV's day, but the Sun King seldom washed. When the bath tub was rediscovered by chance in his successor's time, it was not used to bathe in; la Pompadour had had it set up in the garden for a fountain. The aristocratic style of life was above so elementary a matter as cleanliness, and scent could be used to camouflage smell. Wide staircases, long draughty corridors and galleries and almost unheatable rooms meant that life in the vast Baroque châteaux was far from agreeable. We can well sympathize with the constant complaints recorded during that period about the interminable waiting in cold, dark galleries.

The small Rococo châteaux are better suited to modern requirements – Sanssouci, for instance. Probably the most thorough modernization was that carried out in the Grand Trianon at Versailles; de Gaulle had the building renovated at a cost of more than fifty million francs partly to house guests and partly as a kind of private residence in addition to the Elysée Palace and the hôtel de Rambouillet, the last-named having been at the disposal of French presidents since 1883. This is a case where it is difficult to distinguish between a reversion to former conditions and practical use.

Palaces and châteaux are often occupied by governments, from national bodies down to small local authorities. Prague Castle and the Palazzo di Quirinale in Rome are now the seats of heads of state. And Austrian charm may account for the fact that a registrar now officially blesses unions in Salzburg's Schloss Mirabell, where lawful marriage was denied to the original occupants, an archbishop and his mistress, a commoner.

Thus the castles and mansions of the past four centuries now serve the people of our own day in all the countries of Europe in the most diverse ways. Almost all have sacrificed their exclusivity, but instead have won a host of sincere admirers of the past whose desire is to fashion a present and a future in which beauty and comfort will not be the privilege of an élite, but the natural amenities of human life.

SOURCES OF ILLUSTRATIONS

Front cover:
The Moritzburg near Dresden. Aerial view by L. Willmann, Berlin
Back cover: Versailles, Cabinet de la pendule. By courtesy of Service de documentation photographique de la réunion des musées nationaux, Versailles

Adelmann, Paris: 41
Arkady, Warsaw: 92 left (Jablonski), 90 right, 92 right, 93 (Kupiecki), 94 right (Zborski)
Beyer, Weimar: 72, 73, 75, 79—81, 85, 87, 118, 122 bottom, 123
Bonniers, Stockholm (Studio Sundahl): 101
British Travel Association, Frankfurt am Main: 65, 67, 69
Callwey Verlag, Munich (Schmidt-Glassner): 86, 99 left, 116
Deutsche Fotothek, Dresden: 27, 28, 76

Editura Meridiane, Bucharest: 123
Forman, Prague: 103
Giraudon, Paris: 53
Hahn, Dresden: 82
Interfoto MTI, Bucharest: 125 (Lajos), 127 and 128 (Fényes)
Ittenbach, Berlin: 83
Kunsthistorisches Museum, Vienna: 108
Lavaud, Paris: 54
Martinowski, Prague: 113–115, 117
Musée National du Château de Fontainebleau: 49 left
Novosti, Moscow: 120
Orell Füssli Verlag, Zürich (Probst): 34 right, 36
Österreichische Fremdenverkehrswerbung (Schmeja): 110
Réunion des musées nationaux, Versailles: 57
Rössing, Leipzig: 111, 112
Romanian Travel Association: 129, 130

SCALA, Florence: 23
Schröder-Kiewert, Frankfurt am Main: 30 left, 33, 34 left, 37, 39, 40, 42, 43 left, 47, 51, 52, 53 left, 58, 59, 66, 74, 98, 99 right
Swedish Tourist Office: 97
Sickert, Innsbruck: 21, 22, 24 left, 105, 106
Studio Vista, London: 119 bottom
Süddeutscher Verlag, Munich: 102
Thames & Hudson, London: 25, 26, 31, 32, 70, 71
The Lord Chamberlain's Office, London (H. White): 68
Weidenfeld & Nicolson, London: 43 right (Dundas), 48, 49 right, 60, 61, 95 (all by Graham)
Willmann, Berlin: 84
ZFA, Düsseldorf: 29, 30 right, 35, 38, 44, 45, 50, 55, 56, 62—64, 77, 78, 88, 89, 96, 104, 109, 119 top, 122 top, 126

CONTENTS

ITALY

Of all the countries of Europe, Italy is undoubtedly the richest in historic buildings. Evidence of Roman culture was never quite lost, but it was to have little influence on men's minds until the end of the Middle Ages.

After the pre-Renaissance interlude which was inspired by the Hohenstaufens around the year 1200, the fifteenth century saw an important renewal of architectural activity, particularly in the secular field of commercial, civic and domestic building. Until then the houses of the city patricians had generally been fairly simple. Only the wealthiest merchants had built themselves more luxurious residences with shady arcades on the ground floor, open to the street. These contained shops.

From the word *casa* or house, residences were called "Ca'..." followed by the owner's name; only the residences of rulers, of the mayor and the city prefect were given the name Palazzo, from the Latin *palatium*. It was a name that was to be adopted later for the residences of all influential people.

The vast majority of the palaces built from the end of the fourteenth century until the eighteenth century still survive. By discussing some of the finest examples we shall try to show how the different lines of development were influenced by artistic, political, geographical and climatic factors. As far as Baroque is concerned we have selected a few great houses and

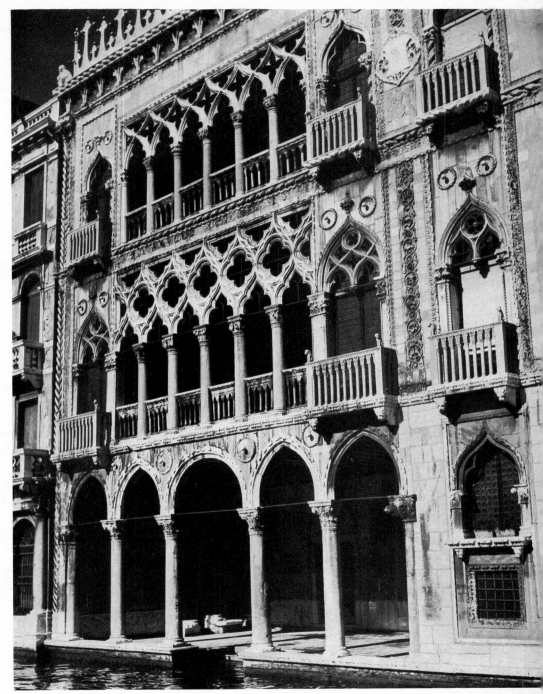

palaces inspired by dynastic ties with France yet in which the Italian artists succeeded in assimilating foreign influence.

In Venice, the great sense of security enjoyed by the inhabitants, both within the city and towards the outside world, determined the form taken by her secular architecture. The ground floors consisted of open arcades giving on to canals and squares; and from the wide arched galleries on the upper floors, the inhabitants could watch everything that went on on the canals, as though from a box in the theatre.

These features have a quite especial charm and beauty in the Ca'd'Oro and The Doge's Palace which was both the seat of government of the Republic of Venice and also the residence of the Doge. On the other hand lack of space in the city made gardens and large courtyards impossible. Since other cities and city-states were not subject to these limitations the architecture of Venice exerted little influence elsewhere.

Florence, where the Medici family on coming to power played a leading part in the encouragement of art, set the standard for the Italian palace; and it was here that the principles of palace architecture mentioned in the introduction were developed. The Medici villas, with their superb gardens, were also largely responsible for the evolution of subsequent landscape gardening.

The palaces were built and decorated with frescos by the most eminent Renaissance artists. Brunelleschi, Mantegna, Botticelli, Raphael, Veronese, Tintoretto and Michelangelo all worked in the palaces of Mantua, Ferrara, Urbino, Florence and Venice. Where they did not use frescos or fine decorations in stucco or choice woods to achieve their spatial effects, the predominant material was marble.

About 1550 the architect Andrea Palladio was working in Venice and Vicenza. His most famous and also his most mature, work

Ca' d'Oro, Venice. The façade of the Ca'd'Oro, like the piazzetta façade of the Doge's Palace by the same architects, shows the last traces of Venetian Gothic. It owes its name – House of Gold – to the rich tracery of the façade which was formerly gilded. The courtyard with its magnificent fountain is held to be the finest in Venice. The house was built between 1421 and 1450. In 1895 it was bought by Baron Fran-

chetti who restored it and later donated it to the state, together with an important art collection. Since then the Ca' d'Oro has been a museum. In accordance with an ancient Venetian tradition, the entrance is situated within the deep, shady arcade on the ground floor.

Doge's Palace, Venice. The first Doge's Palace was built in 814 as the official and

private seat of the head of the Republic, who was elected for life. The palace we see today was built in the fourteenth and fifteenth centuries.

The private apartments, which consist of three small rooms, seem very modest beside the highly decorated staircases and council chambers. Two fine staircases lead from lower to upper floors. The "Giant's Staircase", at whose head the newly elected doges were presented, leads up from the

Doge's Palace, Venice

inner court to the first floor. The Golden Staircase with its rich sculptural decoration leads to the state rooms on the second and third floors.

Paintings by Veronese and Tintoretto adorn the Senate Hall where the Council of Ten received illustrious visitors and upon whose tribune they held their important meetings presided over by the Doge. The Great Council Chamber contains one of the world's largest oil paintings, Tintoretto's Paradiso *which is 74 feet long by 30 feet high. The fourteenth and fifteenth century*

façades, partly broken by arcades with tracery and partly decorated with colored brickwork, are a main feature of the piazza of St. Mark's viewed from the Grand Canal.

Palazzo Ducale, Mantua. The history of the building of this palace, one of the greatest in Italy, is a complex one, for it developed out of a number of older structures. In one tower of the former Castello di San Giorgio there is the Camera degli Sposi, *whose wall-paintings*

is the Villa Rotonda; this is perhaps the clearest example of his style deriving from the Greco-Roman architectural tradition. His influence upon European architecture has already been mentioned.

During the Baroque era Rome took over the artistic and intellectual role of Florence. For although the Medici continued to reign until 1737, their interests had turned to the

make it unique even in Italy. When, in 1474, Mantegna depicted scenes from the life of Lodovico Gonzaga, he created the earliest genuine group portrait known in European art.

Equally remarkable because of its balanced proportions and its unusual architectural form is the great riding-school by Giulio Romano. Under Austrian domination part of the palace was converted in eighteenth and nineteenth century style for the use of the empresses. Today the Palazzo Ducale is owned by the state.

ruthless pursuit of power. The flowering of Rome was not restricted to the geographical limitations that had been imposed on Venice and Florence, hence the palaces of the popes and cardinals could evolve beyond the rigid Florentine plan of a rectangle around a central courtyard.

As one example of the vast Roman Baroque palace, we shall take the Palazzo Barberini, which was built for Pope Urban VIII's family by Carlo Maderna, the architect of the façade of St. Peter's, and his nephew, Borromini. This building was completed by Lorenzo Bernini who had been responsible for the magnificent piazza of St. Peter's, and had helped to give Rome its Baroque character.

The interior effect of the rooms was very largely achieved by the paintings on their walls. Tiepolo was to gain a high rep-

utation as an architectural painter, his works being also found in Germany and Spain. The predilection for marble was growing: the great halls are alive with its wonderful light-reflecting properties, as are the groups of figures in the gardens. This noble material was used even for mangers and partitions in the stables of the Villa Lechi in Brescia and the Villa Pisani near Venice.

Charles III of Naples, a Bourbon and grandson of Louis XIV, commissioned the great Baroque palace at Caserta, firstly because the old Neapolitan residence lay within easy range of the guns of English warships, and secondly because there was insufficient space for a display of splendor on the French or Spanish model. The new residence arose further inland, at Caserta, and was begun in 1752. The most appropriate description is to be found in a letter written by Princess Gonzaga, who called it the 'Versailles of the Kings of Naples'.

An exceptionally original solution was reached, on the other hand, by the theatrical painter and architect, Juvara, for Stupinigi near Turin, which had been planned as a small hunting lodge. Growing beyond what had originally been planned, the building became a monumental structure, with a Rococo version of the high Baroque ground plan, the central portion being oval, with four wings at right angles.

Palazzo Ducale, Urbino. This building, which has been called the "first royal palace of modern times", was begun in 1447. But only twenty years later it was rebuilt and renovated to produce a masterpiece of Renaissance architecture. It was, indeed, famous even while it was still being built. Lorenzo de' Medici and Federico Gonzaga asked for models and architectural drawings. The building reflected the brilliant intellectual and social life at the court of the Montefeltro. The scheme was exceptionally comprehensive, including a library, theatre, riding-school, conservatory, two bathrooms and a cold room in which snow was preserved for the summer. Botticelli was involved in the decoration of the duke's small, but luxuriously furnished, study. However, it was characteristic of this so "enlightened" prince's court that the duchess's bedroom door could only be opened from the outside, so that every night she became a prisoner.

In 1625 the palace was sold to Pope Urban VIII. It now belongs to the state and houses the Galleria Nazionale delle Marche.

Palazzo Medici-Riccardi, Florence. The palace which the architect Michelozzo was commissioned to build in 1440 by Cosimo de' Medici, known as Il Vecchio, became the model for Florentine palaces in the fifteenth century. The bold cornice and also the rustication on the ground floor are

Palazzo Medici-Riccardi, Florence

characteristic features. The ground floor windows of the pediment type in bold semicircular arches were designed by Michelangelo. The palace was the seat of the Medici family until 1537 when Cosimo I moved into the Palazzo Vecchio, the town residence in Florence. In 1659 the palace, now one of the many belonging to the Medici family, was sold to the Riccardi family and was later considerably enlarged by them. Today it contains the offices of the prefecture, but part of it is open to visitors.

The inner courtyard has typical arcaded galleries which formerly were also open on the first **floor.**

Villa Rotonda, Vicenza. Palladio's famous villa was begun for the papal referendary Almerico in 1550. Both patron and architect died before it was completed. The Capra family bought the building and commissioned Scamozzi to complete it. The Rotonda is distinguished from countless other villas by its balanced, strictly symmetrical design based upon a ground plan that is a regular Greek cross, and further by its successful adaptation to its natural setting. All four sides have similar façades, each with six columns, supporting a triangular pediment. Each portico is reached by means of a wide flight of steps.

The Villa Rotonda is today, as it has been for centuries, in the possession of Count Valmarana's family.

Villa Rotonda, Vicenza

Palazzo Reale, Caserta

Palazzo Reale, Caserta. Impelled by the desire to keep up with his grandfather, Louis XIV, King Charles III commissioned the Italian architect Vanvitelli to build the huge palace at Caserta in 1752. The influence of Versailles is particularly evident in the somewhat uninteresting façade on the side facing the city. Yet the great rectangular complex which had to include administrative sections, is admirably organized.

Along the medial axes Vanvitelli built two long wings and where these intersect there is an octagonal hall which is the center point of the whole complex. The interior reflects French taste. An early and well-designed water system

is matched by the luxury of a gold-plated bath and taps.

The layout of the grounds also shows an attempt to outdo Versailles. Extending between the palace and a nearby hill are more than three miles of artificials pools, cascades and waterfalls. Everywhere there are complex sculptural groups, such as that of Diana and Acteon. Part of the palace is now a military academy and the rest houses a museum.

Palazzo Barberini, Rome. This palace was commissioned after 1625 by Pope Urban VIII as a seat for his family. Three masters of Roman Baroque worked on this building. It departs from the principle of the Baroque palace in its design of a main block with two transverse wings. In 1949 the palace was bought by the state; since then it has housed the Galleria Nazionale. The most important work in the gallery is Raphael's Fornarina.

34

Palazzina di Caccia, Stupinigi, near Turin.
The royal hunting lodge begun by Filippo Juvara,
scenery painter and architect, in 1729, creates
the impression of an enormous piece of perspective
stage scenery. Italians did not rate hunting
especially highly, and this palace therefore betrays
French influence. Everywhere there are symbols
of the chase, after the French manner. The
ceiling of the main hall is decorated with a
painting of the triumph of Diana, the goddess
of the chase. The X-shaped location of the
wings connect the main building with later
extensions. Today the hunting lodge belongs to
the Knightly Order of Saints Maurice and
Lazarus.

36

SWITZERLAND

Stockalper Castle, Brig

In Switzerland the landscape outside the towns is dominated by the castles which determined the country's history after the end of the Middle Ages. Many medieval fortified buildings were destroyed in the struggles between the free peasants and the citizens against the nobility who, though themselves of little consequence, were supported by foreign dynasties. Other keeps were destroyed by an earthquake in 1356.

In the early sixteenth century, which saw the heyday of feudal castle architecture in other countries, the rise of the commonalty in Switzerland had brought about the end of foreign intervention, and the cantons already formed a powerful confederation. This explains the absence of great houses; more often, existing castles were converted, and the few genuine palaces were commissioned by bishops or commoners.

Typical of these is the great Stockalper Castle at Brig which was the largest private residence built in Switzerland until the nineteenth century. It was erected by the

Stockalper Castle, Brig. The exterior of this castle, which belonged to the subsequently ennobled import merchant Stockalper, has as its main features three corner towers of five stories, rising high above the domestic wings. These served no real defensive purpose, in spite of the embrasures in the parapets. Until 1949 the castle

belonged to the family of its founder, and then
passed into the possession of the town of Brig.

The inner courtyard of this building erected in
1642 is reminiscent of Italian early Renaissance
models.

Bottmingen Castle. The last well-preserved
waterside castle near Basle was never a seat of
nobility. It belonged to the Bishops of Basle and,
after 1534, to the city of Basle itself. The later
owner, Deucher, who was a commoner, rebuilt
the edifice along Baroque lines in 1720. In 1954 it
was bought by the canton of Baselland, and is
now a restaurant.

Oberhofen Castle. Situated on the banks of Lake Thun this waterside castle, which had already been in existence in the twelfth century, became from the fifteenth century onwards the seat of the Bernese mayors and bailiffs. Subsequently, constant modernization of the living quarters did little to alter the stern austerity of the exterior, until 1844 when the Prussian Lord Master of Ceremonies, Graf von Pourtales, had it altered in romantic historical style. A Turkish living room was installed, for instance, in the twelfth century belfry. After many changes of ownership the castle was presented to the Bernese Historical Museum in 1952. The ancient and valuable fabric of the building was restored, and the castle was opened to the public in 1954. The garden with its rare trees is among the finest in Switzerland.

39

merchant, Stockalper, in 1642 as a residence *cum* warehouse and to provide quarters for the mule trains that carried his goods. Stockalper, who held trade monopolies, also ran a postal service between Geneva and Milan. His castle further served as a barracks for the *Reisläufer* or Swiss mercenaries who, between the sixteenth and eighteenth centuries, sold their services to all the countries of Europe.

The castles and palaces were to experience a further decline during the French Revolu-

tion when, with the help of French revolutionary soldiers, the Swiss Republic was created.

Some Swiss castles were put to a different use at an early date; the Marschlins Castle, for instance, became an educational institution in 1771, when Martin Planta set up his "Philanthropin" there. Forty years later Pestalozzi was to establish his world-famous educational institution at the castle of Yverdon, a fortified edifice like so many others in Switzerland.

Marschlins Castle. This building with its four towers was formerly an ancient waterside castle which was rebuilt in 1633 for Field Marshal Ulysses von Salis along Baroque lines. In 1905 the château was once again converted, this time with historical furnishings and works of art. It is still in private hands.

SPAIN

During the time when Spain still formed part of the Roman Empire she acquired not only the usual theatres, walled towns and aqueducts, but also Augustus' palace at Tarragona. Genuine castles only began to be built with the arrival of the Saracens who occupied the country in the eighth century. All but small sections of the country in the north was soon overrun by the Moors. The Saracenic ruling caste built their palaces in the province of the Caliph of Cordova, and when the disintegration of the kingdom of Cordova in the middle of the thirteenth century gave rise to the kingdom of Granada, the latter became the meeting place for the artists and scholars from the areas of Cordova and Seville conquered by "their most Catholic Majesties" Ferdinand and Isabella. Palaces and pleasure châteaux, with gardens and trick fountains, were expressions of the high flowering of Saracenic domestic culture and civilization, and of these the finest was the Alhambra in Granada, an extensive complex that evolved without plan from a number of individual buildings. The earlier citadel on the hill of Asabica became *Al Qala al-Hambra*, the "red fortress". But the buildings which arose here, against the backdrop of the snow-covered Sierra Nevada, were very far from being military, utilitarian structures. Behind the thick walls there grew up during the fourteenth century ornate, ingeniously decorated pal-

Alhambra, Granada. The Alhambra lies on a plateau above the town of Granada. Most of the buildings are built in oriental style around majestic courtyards whose rich ornamentation testifies to the decorative skill of the Saracenic craftsmen. Little remains of the marvelous coloration of the architecture. Materially contrib-uting to the enchantment of this fairy-tale architecture are countless little streams of water gurgling through courtyards and inner rooms, as well as the sunlight reflected from the marble floors of the shade-giving courtyards onto the intricate forms of the vaulting.

The roof of the Court of the Lions is sup-ported by twelve slender columns of alabaster. In Moorish times the fountain with its twelve stone lions was surrounded with flowers and shrubs.

The Alhambra was captured in 1492 and partly rebuilt as a royal residence which fell into disuse during the eighteenth century. A

aces, courts of audience and seraglios. The finest of these pillared courtyards, the Court of the Lions, has become famous throughout the world as a symbol of Moorish decorative art.

Although the rulers of Christian zones did all they could to check the power of the Moorish kings, both they and their feudal nobility caused their palaces to be built in the richly ornamental Moorish style. The art of these Saracens who, even after the conquest, enjoyed considerable personal and artistic freedom, was to leave its stamp for nearly three hundred years on what was known as the Mudéjar style. Moorish architects were employed especially for the building of palaces, often in conjunction with Christian colleagues, by Christian feudal rulers who eagerly copied the more refined way of life of the Saracenic grandees. The Mudéjar style survived into the sixteenth century, even when the increasing power of the Inquisition compelled Muslims either to renounce their religion or to emigrate.

thorough restoration was undertaken in the nineteenth century.

Charles V's Castle, Granada. The magnificent position and the enchanting architecture of the Alhambra moved Charles V to have a castle built in the immediate vicinity. By 1616

Alcázar, Seville

there was a quadrangular block enclosing a circular courtyard with a two-tiered arcade, so that it resembled an arena. Beside the ornate architecture of the Alhambra, the Italian Renaissance style makes an impression of frigid grandeur. The building was not completed and was never lived in.

Alcázar, Seville. The Alcázar, finest of the Mudéjar palaces, arose in the middle of the fourteenth century. The building was commissioned by Pedro I who employed upon it not only Saracenic architects put at his disposal by his friend, the ruler in Granada, but also Christian master builders from Seville and Toledo. Its most beautiful room is the Hall of the Ambassadors, where the decorations are reminiscent of the Court of the Lions in the Alhambra.

Casa del Labrador, Aranjuez. The castle of Aranjuez was erected to the south of Madrid by an Italian architect to replace a hunting lodge belonging to Charles V. The magnificent park is older than the mid-eighteenth century building, and contains the Casa del Labrador. This pavilion was built towards the end of the eighteenth century, in imitation of the Petit Trianon at Versailles. Both façade and interior testify to the influence of the Pompeian architecture and wall paintings which had then recently been excavated. The park also contains one of the earliest garden theatres in Europe (1622).

44

Casa del Labrador, Aranjuez

Subsequently, however, artistic currents began to penetrate from Burgundy, Flanders and Italy. Yet delight in ornamentation has remained an essential feature of Spanish art right up to the present day.

Moorish forms were eventually abandoned and the Mudéjar style superseded by the Plateresque style. *Platero* is the Spanish word for silversmith, and it is characteristic of this trend in art to treat walls simply as a base on which decorative elements may be applied. The Salamanca region

possesses numerous palaces built in this style.

In 1526 the Emperor Charles V spent some time in Spain which was part of his dominions. After his marriage to Isabella of Portugal he lived for a short while in the Alhambra and ordered the building of a new imperial palace in its immediate vicinity. This structure, which has never been completed, was begun by Machuca, a pupil of Michelangelo, in the Italian Renaissance style.

In 1563 Charles' son, Philip II, commissioned the building of an edifice of vast

proportions in the Escorial near Madrid;
this is a unique combination, so far as
Europe is concerned, of cloister and residence. Philip's successors, weak offshoots
of the house of Habsburg, later forfeited
their power – which even in the case of
Charles V, had been dependent on the
bankers of the houses of Fugger and Welser – almost entirely to the church, and by
degrees Spain ceased to be a world power.
This explains why Baroque architecture in
Spain flourished in only one sphere, that
of monumental church architecture.

*Palace of the Marqués de Dos Aguas, Valencia.
In keeping with the Spanish tradition, the walls
of this building, erected in 1744, form only a
base for the rich ornamental and figurative
decoration around the windows and the white
alabaster entrance. The designer was the painter,
H. Rovira y Broncadel; the sculptor, Ignacio
Vergera. The architectural features are swamped
by the exuberance of the ornamentation and by
sculptured figures, plants and clouds.*

PORTUGAL

Paço Real, Sintra

Seven heraldic "castelos" adorn the Portuguese coat of arms to commemorate the important part played by Portugal's keeps and castles in the reconquest of the land from Moorish rule. The castle of Sintra, which is one of those depicted in the coat of arms, presents an almost complete picture of Portuguese history since Saracenic

Paço Real, Sintra. The exterior of the royal palace is remarkable for its two immense conical kitchen chimneys, which were built about 1400 at the same time as the main rooms.

Within, the rooms are characterized by the use of colored relief tiles and a predilection for painted wooden ceilings.

The Magpie Hall is one of three rooms where the ceilings are decorated with paintings of animals. The choice of subject arose from an episode at court. One day Joao's wife caught him kissing one of the ladies-in-waiting, and it

47

would seem that she was not altogether satisfied with his assurance that "Era por bem" – the intention was honorable. No doubt to admonish the ladies-in-waiting for their inordinate tittle-tattle, the monarch had 136 magpies, one for each of the ladies, painted on the ceiling, with the legend "Por bem".

Queluz Palace (p. 48). Though presenting a sober front, this palace possesses a beautiful Rococo façade on the garden side. Within, French taste manifests itself in the furnishings and combines happily with traditional tiled walls and floors to form a pleasing whole. Even the embankment of a canal in the rustic park is completely clad in colored tiles.

The palace was restored after a fire in 1934 which destroyed several reception rooms, and now part of it is used by the state for official visitors.

In the old kitchen wing a restaurant has been installed, the style matching well with the rest of the building.

Royal Palace, Bussaco (p. 49). "This is where wealthy but unimaginative married couples spend their honeymoon," wrote the author of a book on Portugal. Such, indeed, is the new purpose of the former royal hunting castle erected in 1888, in pseudo sixteenth century Manueline style. It is now the Palace Hotel.

times. The earlier history of the country was closely linked to that of Spain.

The original structure, dating back to the eighth century, was Saracenic. Upon its ruins the new Portuguese dynasty, whose position had been confirmed by the Pope, built a Gothic nucleus around 1400; and during the fifteenth century more rooms were added to the castle, for the prowess of Portugal's navigators, such as Vasco da Gama, had brought increased political significance. The most influential of its owners was Dom John I. One of his successors, Dom Manuel, established what became known, and widely practiced, as the Manueline style, in which the traditional decoration of walls and floors with relief tiles, *azulejos*, was combined with the elements of Spanish Mudéjar and exotic ornamental forms.

The tremendous earthquake of 1755, by which Lisbon was almost razed to the ground, also seriously damaged the castle. However within a few years the latter had been rebuilt. Most of the great houses belonging to the monarchy and to the Lisbon aristocracy were in the Terreiro dos Paços, the terrace of palaces, now the Praça do Commercio, at the very heart of Lisbon. Their destruction, either by the earthquake or by the ensuing floods, served to enhance the importance of Sintra. One of the rooms has been preserved exactly as it was left by the grandmother of the then reigning

monarch when she fled in 1910 on the proclamation of the republic.

During the sixteenth century, the aristocracy began to build summer palaces and villas around the castle, and in the nineteenth century a rival made its appearance – Pena Palace, a dramatically romantic edifice. Indeed, because of its pseudo-medieval appearance, it might almost be called a Portuguese Neuschwanstein, for King Fernando, who commissioned it, came from Coburg, which adjoins Bavaria.

Of infinitely greater charm is the summer palace of Queluz, near Lisbon, started in 1747. Its exquisite coloring and somewhat rustic elegance are characteristic of Portugal, although the palace was designed and its building supervised by a French Rococo architect. Queluz, with its small rooms and gay interiors, is one of the few really habitable great houses of Europe.

During the Hundred Years' War in the fourteenth and fifteenth centuries, large areas of France were under English occupation; and this, together with feuds between rival feudal French nobles, was largely responsible for the fact that, after the flowering of Gothic architecture, the Renaissance did not reach France until almost a hundred years after it had started in Italy.

At the beginning of the fifteenth century the power of the crown was limited to central and south east France, a significant part being played by the Loire district which lay between the two zones occupied by the English.

It was from here that the power of the crown was able to assert itself after the expulsion of the English, and the Loire Valley then became a center of new artistic endeavor in France. It was here that the transition took place from Gothic castle to Renaissance château. The unfortified feudal town residence, the *hôtel*, long continued to be built in the medieval tradition, although the change in the monarchy's social position seemed to call, and to call insistently, for expression in the grandiose and ostentatious building of palaces.

From his travels in Italy, King Charles VIII brought with him artists whom he commissioned to build the Château d'Amboise. Unfortunately the edifice underwent a great many alterations, so that for this time of transition we are obliged to consider only

the later royal palaces and great houses – Blois, Chambord and Fontainebleau. An unmistakable feature that was to persist throughout the Renaissance was the interesting profile resulting from variegated roof forms, decorated chimney stacks and dormer windows, still reminiscent of the profile of turreted castles.

The example set by the royal houses inspired the aristocracy as well as rich commoners who had purchased office and honors. One estate after another appeared in the Loire Valley. Two of these can be regarded as typical of many: Chenonceaux, built for the Superintendent of Finance, Thomas Bohier, on an island in a tributary of the Loire, and Azay-le-Rideau, built for the Treasurer, Gilles Berthelot. Both show the predilection for houses surrounded by water, and this can hardly have been for reasons of safety, so short a distance being no protection against sixteenth century cannon. Clearly the factors under consideration were climatic and aesthetic.

The most richly endowed artistically is Fontainebleau which, by its scattered layout, is not a town residence proper, but in size and importance can only be compared with it. The long halls and galleries almost seem predestined for the activities of artists. The style employed by the Italians Rosso and Primaticcio in their Mannerist plaster decorations and paintings gave its stamp to the "School of Fontaine-

Château de Blois (p. 51). Three adjoining build-ings, all of different dates, flank an irregular courtyard. The original and oldest wing was re-built in its present form between 1635 and 1638. The second wing was built under Louis XII be-tween 1490 and 1503. The third, enclosing the courtyard, was built by Viart during the reign of Francis I between 1515 and 1524. On the

courtyard side of his wing he erected the much admired staircase which spirals upwards inside its open octagonal tower. This house, in which Henri de Guise, the opponent of Henry III, was murdered at the latter's instigation, is now partly open to the public. It also contains a library and two museums of art.

Palace of Fontainebleau. The exterior of the palace, which is built around five irregular courtyards, creates an impression of surprising frigidity. The long façade is an example of the French preference for emphasizing individual pavilions – one reason for the interesting profile of French Renaissance châteaux.

In Francis I's wing the horseshoe stairs built by

Jean du Cerceau project into the Cour des Adieux. *Throughout Europe, they were to be the prototype for the curving Baroque outside staircase.*

By comparison with the well-balanced but distinctly unornate exterior, the main rooms are profusely decorated. Painted and sculptural decoration are at their most luxuriant in the Francis I gallery, *in the ballroom and in the chamber of the Duchesse d'Etampes, later converted into the "King's staircase". Characteristic here are the plaster carvings and ornaments of the Mannerist "School of Fontainebleau".*

Château de Chambord. From 1515 onwards some two thousand workmen were engaged in building the Château de Chambord for Francis I. It was his favorite residence on the Loire. The ground plan is strangely conceived; the square main building and the quadrangular structure which encloses it both recall the castle, each having four round corner towers. The intriguing uniform design of the exterior is carried through in the interior only in the royal apartments.

Most of the four hundred rooms are arranged as individual accommodations for the King's retinue.

Whereas the Château de Blois had been the favorite residence of Queen Claude, Chambord would seem mainly to have served as a place where the King, then a widower, and the gentlemen of his suite could freely indulge their pleasures. What is striking at Chambord is the contrast between the simplicity of the wall surface and the interesting profile of the roofs.

Château de Chenonceaux. The great house, built on an island in the River Cher, is a clear expression of the harmony so popular in France between buildings and surrounding water. The heirs of Bohier, the Superintendent of Finance, had to give the house, which had been begun in 1515, to King Henry II. The King presented it to his mistress, Diane de Poitiers, who commissioned Philibert de l'Orme to connect the building with the farther bank of the river. In 1580

bleau". A colleague of them, the creative French sixteenth century architect, Philibert de l'Orme, wasr esponsible for the façade enclosing the *Cour du Cheval blanc*, named after the plaster cast of the Marcus Aurelius equestrian statue in the Roman Capitol. In the 17th century, Jean du Cerceau placed an outside horseshoe staircase in front of this façade, which was copied by Baroque architects throughout Europe.

Fontainebleau was to know all the monarchs, their courtiers and mistresses up till the time of Napoleon and Louis Philippe. It was here that the Duchesse d'Etampes admired Leonardo's "Mona Lisa", which had been bought by Francis I. History has little to say about the lawful queens who, indeed, with the exception of the ambitious Catherine de Médicis, rarely exerted much influence. Finally, Napoleon stood on the horseshoe staircase when he took leave of his guard after his abdication in 1814. Since then the *Cour du Cheval blanc* has been called the *Cour des Adieux*.

Francis I, the most architecturally minded of rulers, pondered a long time about building a residence fit for a king in the

Jean Bullant, one of the greatest French Renaissance architects, built a long gallery for Catherine de Médicis above the many arches of the bridge. It is this extension that gives the house its unusual character. It is now in private ownership.

Château d'Azay-le-Rideau. This mansion, built between 1518 and 1527, is one of the most unadulterated creations of the early Renaissance in France. Its corner turrets with their conical roofs and its embrasure-like attic windows still

echo the genuine Gothic style. It was the first of the Loire châteaux to possess a straight staircase after the Italian model. It is now a Renaissance museum.

Louvre, Paris. The oldest portion of the Louvre is the southern part of the west wing, in what is known as the Cour Carrée. *This section of the building containing the clock tower was begun under Francis I by Pierre Lescot, and was decorated with reliefs by Jean Goujon. The collaboration of these two artists produced some of the most mature work of the French early Renaissance.*

Château de Vaux-le-Vicomte. This great house was built for the Superintendent of Finance, Fouquet, by a then unknown architect Le Vau. It was completed at vast expense within five years and with the help of an army of 18,000 workmen. It marked the beginning of all the new tendencies in Baroque château architecture. Here for the first time we find the immense suite of rooms and, instead of one central block, individual buildings of various heights, some of them even forming wings separate from the main building. Both these features are copied in Versailles. The influence of the oval salon was persistent and is still found in Rococo architecture.

His eye for artistic talent had enabled Fouquet to engage the men who were to become the masters of the Louis Quatorze style. After arresting its owner, Louis XIV pillaged the house whose furnishings went to embellish Versailles. Part of the marble flooring also found its way to the Louvre. The building is still privately owned, and can only be visited by special permission, but the magnificent grounds are open to the public.

Palace of Versailles. Louis XIV insisted that the plan of the main building should allow for the

capital city. It was not till 1546, a year before his death, that the rebuilding of the Louvre, then a many-towered Gothic castle, began. Pierre Lescot remained in charge of the work until 1578. The later architects continued along the same lines, and in 1665 the minister, Colbert, suggested that Bernini should compete in submitting plans for further building. These were not adopted, however, and the east façade was given a long colonnade. In 1572 the Louvre witnessed the massacre of St. Bartholomew as well as intrigues for possession of the throne. But Louis XIV, who had lived in the Louvre as a child, directed all his energy into realizing his plans for Versailles.

The Louvre was to attain real importance only after 1793 during the Revolution, when the Convention nationalized the royal art collections and put them on public exhibition in the palace. During the nineteenth century systematic additions were made to the collections, and today the Louvre houses one of the greatest exhibitions of art in the world.

With the building of the palaces of Versailles and Vaux-le-Vicomte an epoch began in which France set the standard for the whole of Europe in château architecture. In Louis XIV's time, thirty-six thousand workmen were employed on the whole complex of Versailles. In an unparalleled way, the absolute monarchy concentrated all its financial and artistic resources upon

preservation of the waterside château built by his father between 1631 and 1634. In Le Vau's plan the new palace enveloped the older buildings on three sides. The old château, with its sculptural decorations, still surrounds the Cour de Marbre *today. Versailles received its characteristic stamp from the work of Jules Hardouin-Mansart who rebuilt the palace between 1668 and 1710, when he created the world-famous long*

garden façade. He also extended the building by the addition of wings on either side, to accommodate the officials of the royal household which soon followed the court to Versailles. Hardouin-Mansart's greatest creation, however, was the Galerie des Glaces, which formed a grandiose background for the extravagant court festivities. This great room, 240 feet long, was decorated by Le Brun.

the loftiest of purposes: the glorification of the state.

Since its completion Versailles has in nationalist eyes been the expression of the power and greatness of France. That is why, in 1871, the King of Prussia, William I, had himself crowned German Emperor in Versailles after his victory in the war against France and also why, at the end of the First World War, Germany and Hungary had to sign humiliating peace terms there. For the same reason, too, Charles de Gaulle, on the advice of his Minister of Culture, spent enormous sums on the conversion of the Grand Trianon into accommodations for official guests and as a third residence for himself.

Grand Trianon, Versailles. The Trianon de Porcelaine, built in oriental style in 1670, was replaced by the Grand Trianon designed by Hardouin-Mansart; it is the most elegant building in the whole Versailles complex. It was not intended for the conduct of state business and its form manifests its true function; the separate apartments built for the King and Madame de Maintenon are linked by a covered arcade. Subsequent occupants were Madame de Pompadour, Madame du Barry and Marie-Antoinette.

After the recent costly conversion, official royal visitors will be able to sleep in the beds once occupied by the most famous ladies of France. Parts of the château are open to visitors.

NETHERLANDS
AND LUXEMBOURG

The history of the countries we are now in the habit of describing *en bloc* as Benelux, a name formed from their initial syllables, has been characterized by constant alliances and partitions. The Celtic tribes united to fight the Romans; in the ninth century the area became split up with the division of the Empire; during the Middle Ages it was a continuous bone of contention between England and France because of its prosperous urban economy; under Habsburg rule, it amalgamated to become the Spanish Netherlands, after which the revolt of the northern provinces against Spanish tyranny divided South from North. But in 1814 the whole area was united in the Kingdom of

Binnenhof, The Hague. The Hague, called in Dutch 's Gravenhage, is the seat of the Queen and of parliament. The palace of Binnenhof was built between the fifteenth century and 1700 in Dutch Renaissance style on the site of the castle of the Counts of Holland; at times it served as a residence for the governor.

In the courtyard of the palace, which is now used as the center of government, there is the free-standing thirteenth century Gothic structure of the Hall of the Knights. Every September the state carriage drives into the courtyard bringing the monarch to open the new parliamentary session. The parade of the royal guard also takes place in the Binnenhof.

63

the Netherlands; in 1830 Belgium seceded and became an independent kingdom, and in 1890 the Grand Duchy of Luxembourg also achieved independence. Today there are politicians who like to see the alliance of these countries under NATO as the model for a "united Europe".

Huis ten Bosch, The Hague. Huis ten Bosch is one of the residences of the Dutch royal family. Originally this was the Orange Saloon built as a summer seat for the wife of the governor, William of Orange. The charming, colored brick building was erected by Peter Post and Jacob van Campen on the Palladian model. In 1700 the residence was enlarged and altered, and in 1813 it was acquired by the state for the use of the royal family.

Huis ten Bosch contains two intimate Chinese and Japanese cabinets, as well as the Orange Saloon, two stories high, which is full of portraits as well as paintings of allegorical scenes.

For our purpose, the area begins to acquire interest only in the sixteenth century. The majority of the great houses described in tourists' guidebooks are in fact fortified structures, some of which were made more habitable during the fifteenth and sixteenth centuries. The influence of the native aristocracy was curbed by the early development of the bourgeoisie, and the hallmark of the area's architecture is the civic building of the wealthy towns; the cloth halls, the meat markets and the splendid town halls are infinitely finer than the few genuine mansions belonging to the nobility who, according to religion and estate, sided with the towns against the Spaniards or *vice versa*.

Things did not change very much with the restoration of the monarchy in these countries. Some great houses were built, and ostentatious buildings such as Amsterdam

*Soestdijk Palace. The palace of Soestdijk is
situated between Amersfoort and Amsterdam.
In 1937 the state restored the seventeenth century
hunting lodge and presented it to the royal family.
The simple building lies in a beautiful park
which is open to the public.*

Grand Ducal Palace, Luxembourg

Town Hall were converted into palaces, but these structures remain inherently bourgeois. There are no vast Baroque edifices; besides the few surviving Renaissance châteaux of the aristocracy there are the royal estates whose houses have an essentially domestic character.

Two of Holland's great houses have figured in the history of the past decades. In 1899 Queen Wilhelmina put her royal estate of Huis ten Bosch near The Hague at the disposal of the first World Peace Conference; and in 1919 the Kaiser, William II, abdicated and fled from the revolutionary events in Germany to Count Bentinck's house at Amerongen.

Grand Ducal Palace, Luxembourg. Until 1867 Luxembourg possessed one of the strongest fortresses in Europe and was often called the "Gibraltar of the North". The Grand Duke's palace was built in the sixteenth century and still retains Gothic details. Many illustrious visitors have been to the palace, including Louis XIV and Napoleon. Part of it is now used for sessions of the Luxembourg parliament and part as a residence for the grand ducal family.

67

Hampton Court, near Kingston-upon-Thames. The west front with its large restored gatehouse is in the Tudor style of Cardinal Wolsey's time. The interior of the older part is well preserved. Especially fine is the wooden tracery vaulting with its carved pendants in the great hall where Henry VIII gave his banquets. The former private apartments of the Cardinal are decorated with wall paintings and have fine coffered ceilings.

By looking at the palace from the grounds near the Thames, it is possible to see the point at which Tudor and Baroque meet, the latter being Wren's work whose general effect derives from Versailles.

68

The most fruitful time for the building of
great houses in England was of under-
standably short duration. As the Middle
Ages drew to a close the great nobles
were decimating each other in the Wars of
the Roses between the houses of York and
Lancaster. This materially facilitated the
development of the middle classes. The
turbulent times demanded protective keeps,
not defenseless, luxurious houses. When
the wars were over and a new Tudor king
sat on the throne, only very few of the
high nobility – the potential builders of
great mansions – still remained, and these
were forced to assert themselves in the face
of the lesser landed aristocracy favored
by the king and of the ever more powerful
burghers. The only people to commission
houses of any size were therefore the kings
and the most influential statesmen, such as
Cardinal Wolsey in the time of Henry VIII
and the Duke of Marlborough under
Queen Anne. The new landed aristocracy,
with its many ramifications, either built
comparatively small mansions or modernized older castles.

The victory of Parliament over the monarchy in the Civil War (1642–49) paved the
way for capitalist development. The Lord
Protector, Oliver Cromwell, pursued a
policy which laid the foundations of
Britain's later colonial empire. Although
the monarchy was restored with the House
of Stuart in 1660, its duties were largely

Windsor Castle, Berkshire. Windsor is a unique combination of royal palace, fortress, church and mausoleum. Undeterred by the influx of tourists, thirteen retired senior officers, representatives of the Knights of the Order of the Garter, still regularly attend services in the chapel. King Edward III founded the Order in 1347 at Windsor Castle.

The royal apartments are housed in the wings of the Upper Ward. They owe their Gothic character to nineteenth century restoration.

The massive Round Tower separates the domestic section from the famous St. George's Chapel, which was built during the fifteenth century in perpendicular style. In the choir of the chapel are the tombs of the Kings of England.

70

ceremonial, the country's policy being decided by Parliament. English royalty was virtually precluded from building Baroque mansions, for the sober mood of Parliament and the Treasury would never have permitted the expenditure of vast sums such as were paid out at their subjects' expense by the absolute monarchs of France, Russia and Austria for the building of palaces. They were thus restricted to re-building and modernizing existing residences, such as Windsor Castle.

In Scotland, the extinction of the reigning dynasty in 1286 brought constant feuds among the nobility. This, and the repulse of English claims, necessitated the building of strong keeps right up to 1700. The Highlands were covered with a network of these castles, some of which have been rebuilt and modernized, while the rest have fallen into ruins. Only in very few Scottish castles did domestic comfort take precedence over defense during the sixteenth and seventeenth centuries. Among these is Glamis which, according to local tradition, was the place where its owner, Macbeth, Thane of Glamis, murdered King Duncan. The house built to replace the old castle between 1578 and 1621 shows an unusually late survival of traditional forms, for it is a Gothic castle. This adherence to national characteristics is also found south of the border. For though Renaissance art and culture reached Eng-

land around 1550 and persisted for perhaps another hundred years, Tudor buildings were still being put up until the beginning of the nineteenth century in the latest variant of English Gothic.

The Tudor style is also evident in the impressive palace of Hampton Court on the bank of the Thames. Cardinal Wolsey, Henry VIII's First Minister, began the building but, falling into disgrace in 1529, sought in vain to retrieve his position by presenting the palace to the king. The latter considerably enlarged the building. After 1688 the most eminent architect in the country, Christopher Wren, planned a complete reconstruction of the palace in his own special style, which was a mixture of Baroque and Classical Palladian. His plan was only partially executed so that the two main sections of Hampton Court today reveal England's two most fruitful architectural styles. The most important English contribution to château architecture during the eighteenth century – the "English" park – has already been dealt with in the introduction.

Anyone wishing to visit the royal palaces must naturally take into account the possible presence of the royal family who, however, spend most of the year at their London residence, Buckingham Palace. At Easter time, and during Ascot week, the state rooms at Windsor revert to their original social purpose and cannot therefore be visited by sightseers. On the other hand, some of the landed aristocracy, which are notorious everywhere for their conservatism, open their houses to visitors occasionally for an entrance fee. Really quite an endearing trait.

Blenheim Palace, Oxfordshire. This vast and ostentatious palace was built for the Duke of Marlborough after 1710 by one of the most famous dramatists of his time, Sir John Vanbrugh, who became an architectural dilettante at the age of thirty-six. Blenheim Palace was his first and most famous work. His ebullient dramatic temperament is evident in his new sphere of activity, and the extreme plasticity in the arrangement of architectural features, reminiscent of Italian Baroque, was a breakaway from England's somewhat stiff Palladianism. The vast number of people who visit Blenheim are less interested in the famous dramatist who built it, or in its founder, the Duke of Marlborough, than in seeing the birthplace of Winston Churchill, who was the latter's descendant.

Glamis Castle, Angus (p. 74). During the nineteenth century the visitor to Glamis might still be shown the bed in which the Thane, Mac-

Glamis Castle, Angus

beth, was said to have treacherously slain Duncan, his king. In actual fact, Duncan fell in battle and his place was taken by Macbeth. That bed has now gone, but the legend of the king's death at Glamis has long persisted. Shakespeare may have gotten the idea for Lady Macbeth from

the fate of the mistress of the castle, Janet Douglas, who was burned in Edinburgh in 1537 for alleged witchcraft and high treason. Of the old castle surrounded by legend only a section of the old tower was included in the central block that was built between 1578 and 1671.

Inveraray Castle, Argyllshire. Beside Loch Fyne, which cuts deep into the land, lies the ancient seat of the lords of Argyll. In 1746 a regular building was put up for the Third Duke by Roger Morris and William Adam in place of the fifteenth century castle, but after a fire in

74

Inveraray Castle, Argyllshire

1877, a Gothic exterior was added, including crenellations and conical roofs on the towers. What is, for Scotland, a rich interior derives partly from the Georgian period at the end of the eighteenth century and partly from the late Victorian.

GERMAN
DEMOCRATIC
REPUBLIC
GERMAN
FEDERAL REPUBLIC

Nowhere in Germany can the transition from castle to château be seen more clearly than in the Albrechtsburg, near Meissen. When rebuilt in 1480 the castle was given beautiful vaulted rooms and great Gothic windows, and unity was observed in the treatment of the stories. Thus already many of the domestic requirements of the château had been fulfilled. After this promising start, however, the majority of German feudal lords were prevented from building great houses by the Reformation and the Peasants' War, though many of their castles were destroyed during battles with the rebellious peasants. The Protestant princes, however, were more favorably situated: on the one hand they were able to lay their hands on the property of the secularized monasteries in their provinces, and on the other they were spared the depredations of the Peasants' War. Thus early Renaissance château building in Germany was largely confined to Saxony. The wealth acquired by the Wettin dynasty from the silver mines and the monasteries enabled them to begin rebuilding their residence in Dresden and to start work on a new château at Torgau, Schloss Hartenfels. French influence is generally in evidence in these buildings.

No sooner had the princes and the lesser nobility consolidated their position after the defeat of the peasants than medieval castles began everywhere to give way to

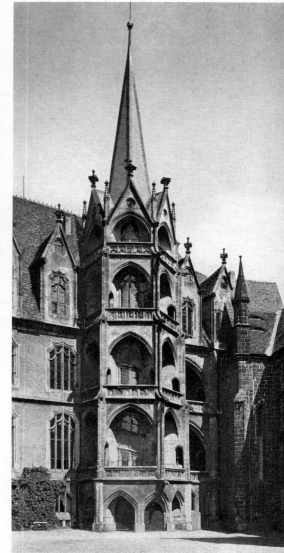

Albrechtsburg, Meissen. From the Elbe Valley the complex on the hilltop, consisting of the cathedral and the ducal and episcopal palaces, has the appearance of a genuine fortified structure. The frontage on the courtyard with its great stone spiral staircase and the tall bay windows are no longer those of a castle, however, nor are the skillfully constructed vaulted ceilings within.

The architect, Arnold of Westphalia, applied all available artistic and technical skills to the building of the ducal palace, the first real domestic residence in Germany – though it was never to serve as such.

From 1710 until 1865 the palace housed the porcelain factory, at first under the management of the inventor of European porcelain, Johann Friedrich Böttger. Today the principal rooms are open to visitors while part of the palace is a museum for Saxon art.

châteaux. There would seem to have been a general trend that led from fortified building, through domestic architecture, to that of ostentatious splendor, while ground plans show a development from the irregular to the symmetrical castle form. The early manifestations of ornate façades are nearly always turned inwards, as at Meissen, towards the courtyard, and only very seldom do they face outwards, towards the adjacent town. At Heidelberg Castle the various

Schloss Heidelberg. Palace of the Counts Palatine. The palace, which arose from a medieval castle above the Neckar, is like a textbook of German Renaissance architecture when viewed from the courtyard. Between 1544 and 1615, four completely distinct Renaisssance buildings were put up by different owners – the "Glass Saloon Building", the "Ottheinrich Building", the "Friedrich Building" and the "English Building". Whereas the Glass Saloon Building with its ponderous forms is reminiscent of Romanesque architecture, the Friedrich Building to the left of it has a façade richly decorated with figures, indicating the extent to which the German Renaissance was still permeated by Gothic ideas. Between 1689 and 1693 the house was severely damaged by French troops and was partially restored during the nineteenth century. The Friedrich Building contains a collection of portraits, architectural sculpture and arts and crafts.

wings built by successive owners are ranged around the courtyard without any attempt at interrelation, just like medieval houses around a square. Many of the innumerable great houses built after 1550 have courtyard fronts with arcaded galleries, after the Italian model.

Special architectural characteristics are to be found in Protestant private chapels, more especially in central Germany – at Torgau, Augustusburg and Schmalkalden, for instance – for in the absence of larger ecclesiastical buildings at this time the chapels are representative of church architecture generally. Moreover, château architecture was then attracting all the artistic talent of the period and was, indeed, during the sixteenth century, the main province of architecture. The end of the Renaissance is manifested in the rebuilding of the castle at Aschaffenburg at the beginning of the seventeenth century, where the effect is no longer aimed inwards, the fine façades being on the fronts facing the town. This already gives evidence of a Baroque mentality.

Yet for nearly the whole of the first half of the new century, all major building projects were inhibited by the Thirty Years' War. After the Peace of Westphalia there was, indeed, a certain amount of domestic building; but the princes, though they alone had emerged profitably from the murderous war, did not begin building with enthusiasm until the seventeenth century was nearly over.

Because of the vast number of spiritual and secular rulers, efforts were not concentrated in Germany, as they were in France, upon large, individual projects; everyone, down to the poorest and most insignificant princeling, sought to create his own "Versailles" where he could live up to the new princely domestic style and indulge in court ceremonial. Great and small potentates alike acquired a passion for building that went far beyond any practical domestic needs and in which they often visibly competed with their neighbors, selfishly converting the taxes paid by their under-privileged middle-class subjects. They also exploited the labor of the common people, to their own ends, for the unbridled indulgence of their life of pleasure.

In some of the larger towns there were also influential merchants who sought to vie with the aristocracy. As in the case of their noble prototypes, their names have been remembered solely because they built delightful châteaux. Even if they had not built great houses, Louis XIV and Prince Eugene would have been important men; but who would remember the merchant, Richter, were it not for his house at Leipzig-Gohlis, or Carl Theodore of the Palatinate, were it not for Schloss Benrath?

The finest Baroque and Rococo palaces

Schloss Sankt Johannisburg, Aschaffenburg

and houses arose in Berlin and Potsdam, around Dresden and Munich, and again in some of the episcopal sees in the Rhine and Main valleys. In these ecclesiastical electoral principalities, the family of the Counts of Schönborn were able to appoint eleven bishops in the course of one century. During that time the latter either occupied or built as many as fifteen residences, from small "pleasure houses" such as Favorité near Mainz, to huge Baroque palaces such as Würzburg and Pommersfelden which, like Schloss Gaibach, are still in the possession of the Schönborn family. The episco-

Schloss Sankt Johannisburg, Aschaffenburg. Johann Schweickardt von Cronburg, Archbishop of Mainz, and hence the leading German electoral prince, commissioned Georg Riedinger in 1604 to build a new summer residence in the place of the castle which had been destroyed. The new building retained the former ground plan of the castle, but the façades are on the town side; after the Baroque fashion it was the exterior of the building that was intended to impress. At the beginning of the nineteenth century the archbishopric was dissolved, and between 1840 and 1848 the new ruler, Ludwig I of Bavaria, added another building in the form of a Pompeian house, the Pompeianum. Both buildings were gutted by fire in 1945 but have since been restored. The residence houses the state art collection.

pal palace at Würzburg possesses the most splendid and grandiose staircase to be found in German Baroque, and the ceilings are magnificently painted by Tiepolo.

Augustus the Strong had a Rococo palace built at Pillnitz even before the style was generally current in Europe. Pillnitz is also one of the most charming examples of the chinoiserie of the early eighteenth century. By the time Sanssouci was built, Rococo was already beginning to flag, and the more advanced architectural ideas are not evident in the palace as such, but in the already Classical idiom of the colon-

Mespelbrunn Hunting Lodge. The little residence of Mespelbrunn lies not far from Aschaffenburg in a romantic woodland landscape in the foothills of the Spessart Mountains. The family of Echter von Mespelbrunn began the building in 1551, and not long afterwards it was converted into a hunting lodge. It stands mirrored in its own small lake like a picture in a book of fairy tales.

nades. But in building the Neues Palais for purposes of display, Frederick II of Prussia, who liked to consider himself "enlightened", was sadly lagging behind his times.

The first man to apply Classical principles consistently to château architecture was Friedrich Wilhelm von Erdmannsdorff. Baroque forms are wholly absent from the house at Wörlitz built by him, a small residence with the façade of a Greek temple, standing in a landscaped "English" park which contains neo-Gothic and romantic structures. This, the earliest example of German Classicism, was also the last of the

Episcopal Palace, Würzburg. The residence of the Bishops of Würzburg was built between 1720 and 1744 from plans by Johann Balthasar Neumann. It bears all the attributes of a provincial ruler's ostentatious château. Both on the garden side and in front the two wings have been given emphasis by the addition of oval pavilions. The south wing contained the domestic apartments of the Schönborn family, the diningroom being in the pavilion; it is decorated with wall paintings on the Pompeian model. The most impressive part of the house is the vast staircase well with the magnificent double flight of stairs, its ceiling decorated by Tiepolo with gorgeously colored paintings.

châteaux of true artistic merit. The few impressive residences to be built in the nineteenth century were inspired by the romantic and nostalgic fantasies of a handful of unrealistic rulers with tottering thrones. One of these was Ludwig II of Bavaria, whose medley of styles at Neuschwanstein and Linderhof aroused serious doubts as to his state of mind. Nevertheless Linderhof at least, however disjointed the style of its individual features, is an interesting late example of European château architecture and should be visited if only for the setting to which it has been so finely adapted.

Amalienburg Hunting Lodge, Munich-Nymphenburg. In the park of Schloss Nymphenburg, built by Prince Max Emmanuel of Bavaria, François Cuvilliés built the hunting lodge of Amalienburg during the years between 1734 and 1739. It was commissioned by Carl Albrecht and Anna Amalia, both of whom loved hunting in the well-stocked woods around Nymphenburg. The princess used to shoot pheasants from the flattened roof of the dome above the one-story building. The necessary offices are situated in two small wings on either side of the living rooms which have rich Rococo decoration in delicately colored plaster. In one of the wings is the small kitchen, its walls covered in colored Delft tiles.

Schloss Pillnitz

Moritzburg Hunting Lodge. The former ducal hunting lodge situated near Dresden acquired its present appearance when in 1723 Augustus the Strong commissioned his architects Pöppelmann and Longuelune to rebuild that old sixteenth century building. The four low, massive corner towers were linked with the enlarged center block and were given Baroque features. Around the house, with its compact structure, terraces and slopes were laid out and planted with trees. The lake around the whole was artificially enlarged. The house is now a Baroque museum, some of the rooms still retaining their beautiful furnishings. Items of especial value are the leather and exotic feather tapestries. In the banqueting hall there is a fine collection of antlers.

Schloss Pillnitz. In 1720 Augustus the Strong commissioned the same architects to build his "Indian pleasure château" beside the Elbe. Three years later its twin, the Bergpalais, was built. With its strangely shaped roofs and painted friezes of Chinese figures and scenes, Pillnitz has won admiration as an example of the chinoiserie that so delighted the eighteenth century; its playful elegance makes it an early work of German Rococo. Today the palace is used principally for crafts exhibitions.

Schloss Sanssouci, Potsdam

Schloss Sanssouci, Potsdam. Frederick II, usually known as the Great, moved the Prussian court from Berlin to nearby Potsdam. There, in a vineyard beside the Havel River, he commissioned one of his friends, the officer-engineer Knobelsdorff, to build a small summer palace which won fame in Europe mainly because of its lavish decorative features. Steps lead up from the Great Fountain through six glazed terraces to the palace on the hilltop which, as one ascends, keeps appearing and disappearing from view. Most of its rooms have an intimate, homely character that is very different from the chilly splendor of many Baroque châteaux. This they owe to the gay, and partly gilded, ornate stucco decorations on the walls and ceilings and to the warm colorfulness of silk tapestries.

In the visitors' wing the Voltaire Room, decorated with naturalistic paintings of animals, fruits and flowers, recalls the three consecutive years spent by the philosopher at Sanssouci.

In the large grounds which, at the beginning of the nineteenth century were partially converted into an English park by the landscape gardener Lennée, there are a number of other buildings such as the Orangery, a picture gallery and a Chinese teahouse. At the end of the park's main axis is the Neues Palais, which impresses more because of its size and its outmoded display of grandeur than by any real artistic originality. Worthy of mention, however, is the theatre in the Neues Palais, which can barely seat three hundred yet which is lent a festive air by the gilded decorations and its form as an amphitheatre.

Schloss Wörlitz. The first great Classicist house in Germany was built between 1769 and 1773 by F. W. von Erdmannsdorff for the Princes of Anhalt-Dessau. It was inspired by Erdmannsdorff's travels in England and Italy. The grounds were landscaped at the same time, to become the first "English garden" on German soil. The two-story building now serves as a museum. It contains many excavated objects from classical times and also paintings, more especially by Dutch masters of the seventeenth century.

Schloss Linderhof. Behind the single neo-Baroque façade are a number of smaller buildings which arose one by one and were then linked together. Ludwig II of Bavaria, an admirer of Wagner, had at first imagined a gigantic building in Byzantine style, but then decided on a large copy of Versailles such as had been erected at Herren Chiemsee. But essentially Linderhof is like the Petit Trianon. The splendor of the interior often borders on vulgarity, but the exterior, and particularly the façade, is in interesting contrast to the surrounding mountain scenery.

POLAND

Under the rule of Kings Sigismund I and Sigismund Augustus, Poland attained a state of prosperity which enabled the culture of the Renaissance to flourish until the middle of the sixteenth century. At this time the royal residence was at Kraków, and after the succession of Sigismund I the rebuilding of Kraków Castle on the Wawel was begun. Thirty years earlier the castle at Debno had undergone the transition from the defensive to the predominantly domestic. From his brother's court at Buda, the king brought Florentine artists back to Kraków where the ancient building was subjected to a thorough-going reconstruction. Its Renaissance forms, and particularly the arcaded galleries on the courtyard side, confirm its Italian origins. A similar process took place at the Piast princes' castle at Brzeg where Italian builders created a residence richly decorated with sculpture. Nothing of this remained after the Prussian siege of 1741 except the series of ducal portraits on the gatehouse. During the final part of the sixteenth century, the Polish magnates, or higher nobility, were able increasingly to curtail the rights of the

Royal Palace, Kraków

monarchy; indeed, after 1572 they usually saw fit to elect to the Polish throne foreign princes who would leave the real government of the country in their own hands.

This period saw the building of noteworthy palaces for the nobility, more especially in Warsaw which had been the capital since 1596. Among the architects, most of them foreigners, who had settled in Poland, the most eminent at this time was Tylman van Gameren. The seventeenth century is characterized by the retention of Renaissance principles, as at Krzyztopor where, between 1631 and 1644, a pentagonal château arose upon fortified bastions; the emphasis on corner towers, adopted

Royal Palace, Kraków. On an eminence known as the Wawel beside the Vistula lies what used to be the royal residence. This comprises the buildings of the old castle, the cathedral and the Renaissance château built by Italian architects after 1502. Between 1531 and 1535 the Florentine architect Berecci added two-tiered arcaded galleries around the courtyard, thus rendering it more than ever Italianate. Of all the rooms in the Renaissance building, the finest and most beautiful is the Hall of the Ambassadors, com-

Debno Castle

from earlier defensive structures, was indeed to remain, if only in a purely aesthetic capacity, a feature of architecture until well into the eighteenth century.

Only in eastern Poland did the towers retain some of their old defensive function because of the proximity of Russia and the Ukraine, parts of which were

pleted between 1529 and 1535, where Polish kings used to receive their guests. In the coffers on the ceiling there are carved heads which seem to be looking down on the ceremonies below as though they would like to take part in them.

Under Austrian rule the Wawel served as a barracks, and it was only at the turn of the century that nationally minded circles raised sufficient funds to redeem it from the military authorities.

In 1961 the valuable figured tapestries that had been part of the former Wawel treasure, and also the crown jewels, were sent back to Kraków from Canada and are now on view.

Debno Castle. Debno lies to the north of the confluence of the Oder and Warta Rivers. The small residence built there in 1480 shows the transition in Poland from castle to château. The ground plan still follows the principle of a fortified structure, but above the rubble walling of the plinth, the corner towers and walls are carried out in soft brick facings. The large windows on the ground floor are a sure sign that the house was built for domestic purposes and not for defense.

Castle of the Piasts, Brzeg
Royal Palace, Wilanow

Castle of the Piasts, Brzeg. The somewhat unsophisticated portraits of Piast dukes in the ancestral gallery are delightful examples of vernacular art. After 1741 the building was used as a depot. In recent years a museum has been set up in the surviving Renaissance hall.
Royal Palace, Wilanow. The pleasure palace was intended to be a modest villa for King John III Sobieski, but shortly after 1680 the plans were considerably expanded. In about 1730 the house was modernized and partly refurnished.

Today Wilanow contains an arts and crafts collection, a small picture gallery and a poster exhibition. Some of the rooms are now open to visitors. The stucco decorations in King John Sobieski's state bedroom were created by Andreas Schlüter in 1692.

occupied from time to time by Poland. Elsewhere they were used solely for artistic effect, as in the episcopal palace at Kielce erected between 1637 and 1641, where they are connected by long galleries to the main building.

As the seventeenth century wore on, the houses of the magnates increased in height, and hardly anything remained to recall their former defensive character which had made way for the Baroque plan of a primary center block with low transverse wings.

In 1697 Augustus the Strong of Saxony had succeeded with the support of Austria in obtaining the Polish crown, after he had adopted the Roman Catholic faith and

expended enormous sums in bribes. He subsequently attempted to bolster up his somewhat shaky position by means of favoritism and a display of splendor and ostentatious building projects. To this end he set up a building department in Warsaw similar to the Court Building Office in Dresden to take care of the planning and execution of building projects. Thus alongside the architectural tradition carried on by the magnates, an alien, Saxon trend was introduced, without, however, exercising any appreciable influence. The main results of these efforts were the rebuilding of the royal palace in Warsaw, the laying out of a new axis through the city, a number of town palaces, and the rebuilding of the

palace of Wilanow near Warsaw, originally built in the middle of the seventeenth century. In 1732 Augustus paid an official visit to the "newly repaired and finely furnished pleasure château". Towards the middle of the century the Saxon episode came to a sudden end. But the magnates continued to build even after 1791 when the "Interminable Diet" had put an end to their political supremacy. There were purely Baroque houses, built around a *cour d'honneur*, such as Rogalin, as well as single blocks on the Palladian model, usually with a cupola over the main hall. Genuine Classicism was also quickly adopted, though at Natolin it is combined with Rococo elements. The greatest achievement was,

perhaps, Domenico Merlini's "Palace on the Water" in the Lazienki Park in Warsaw. Schinkel's romantic palace at Kornik, a mixture of Gothic and Classical styles, marks the culmination of château and palace building in Poland. In the brutal devastation of Warsaw, the royal palace and all others of any importance were destroyed. Many of them have been reconstructed, however, and have been put to new uses.

97

Natolin Palace. This small palace, built between 1780 and 1782, presents an unusual combination of Rococo features, such as the oval saloon with its cupola and open arcade on the garden side, and of Classicist architectural forms.

"Palace on the Water", Warsaw. During the last quarter of the eighteenth century Domenico Merlini combined a number of small palaces and pavilions into an ensemble in Lazienki Park for King Stanislaus Augustus Poniatowski. Around the earlier, circular bath house (lazienki-bath), he built the wholly Classical Palais Na Wodzie (On the Water), which, with its small but valuable art exhibition, is again open to visitors now that the severe war damage has been repaired. The palace and its park are a place of recreation for the people of Warsaw.

Kronborg Castle (p. 99). From this stronghold the Danish King Erik used to exact dues from ships passing through the Sound in the fifteenth century. In 1577 the Flemish fortifications engineer, Anthonis van Opbergen, replaced the fortress with a quadrangular castle, corner towers and bastions. Its fortified nature gave it a sterner appearance than that of other great houses built at this time.

The interior is simple but contains valuable works of art and furnishings, for since 1922 Kronborg has been a museum. The Hamlet festivals take place in the castle yard.

Vadstena Castle. Gustav Vasa began the conversion of the castle beside the Vätter Lake into a Renaissance château in 1545. His marriage was solemnized there. Building went on until 1620, so permitting a more liberal application of Renaissance forms as they gradually became assimilated in Sweden. After the end of the seventeenth century Vadstena ceased to be a residence and was used as a grainery for almost a hundred years until it was restored by the state in 1860.

Gripsholm Castle. Beside a bay on the southern shore of Mälar Lake stands the old family castle of Gustav Vasa, who had the building modernized between 1537 and 1544 by Hendrik von Cöllen, whom he brought from Germany. It was at Gripsholm that Gustav Vasa kept his modest art collection and now the castle, restored in 1900, contains a fine collection of historic portraits, furniture, and valuable Gobelin tapestries. In 1782 Gustav III built a small theatre which, in spite of the Classicist dignity of its interior, still possesses the intimate atmosphere of a Baroque court theatre.

Until 1523 the countries of Denmark, Sweden and Norway were united under the Union of Kalmar. With the secession of Sweden, which became an independent kingdom under the rule of Gustav Vasa, Scandinavia split up into two spheres of influence – Sweden together with Finland on the one hand, and Denmark, to which Norway remained subject till 1814, on the

Frederiksborg, near Hilleröd. In 1560 the Danish king Frederik II laid the foundation stone for the castle to be built upon small islands in Frederiksborg Lake; the buildings, however, mostly date from the years between 1602 and 1621. For a century Frederiksborg remained a royal residence, but for many years after that it continued to be regarded as the country's principal seat. Frederik VII was proposing to restore it to its former status when it was completely gutted by fire in 1859. Virtually all that was left was the old Protestant chapel, where the kings had formerly been crowned. It contains a magnificent organ built in 1610. Frederiksborg was rapidly rebuilt and turned into a national history museum.

other. In both countries the rule of an aristocratic monarchy provided conditions favorable to the building of houses and palaces; and since this was often the responsibility of Dutch or German architects, external influence was considerable.

In these countries castles were almost invariably either adjacent to or surrounded by water. The transition from castle to château took place about the middle of the sixteenth century. In Denmark, the fortified château of Kronborg replaced the castle where, according to Shakespeare, the tragedy of "Hamlet, Prince of Denmark" once took place. Although the account by the chronicler, Saxo Grammaticus, from which the legend derives, is known to be dubious, it has, of course, been

Drottningholm Palace. Hedwig Eleonora, Charles X's widow, built this summer residence, the first Baroque château in Sweden, on Lovö Island in Mälar Lake in 1662. The park at Drottningholm (Queen's island) was also the first great Baroque garden in Scandinavia.

In 1762 the palace theatre was burned down, but within four years it had been replaced by a new, late Baroque building with an auditorium of unique design. The area immediately in front of the stage was reserved for the royal couple, who sat in the front row instead of in a box, and for the highest circles at court; the seats for the nobility lay immediately behind them. During the summer operas by Handel and Gluck are performed in this theatre.

Royal Palace, Stockholm. The castle, Tre Kronor, *which lay at the very heart of Stockholm, on the island of Staden, could not adequately represent the glory of a great power such as Sweden in the time of Charles XI. Its transformation was already planned when a fire in 1697 necessitated a complete rebuilding. Nicodemus Tessin the Younger, who had studied in Italy, erected a vast Baroque palace of which the Italianate exterior is in interesting contrast to the decorations within, carried out by French Rococo artists.*

Gustav III who, by a coup d'état, had made himself an absolute monarch, behaved more "democratically" in the sphere of art; in 1792 he founded the "royal museum", placing some of the royal art treasures on exhibition and giving access to them by special entrances into the palace.

Gustav III was the first of the Swedish monarchs to take an interest in archaeology. He set up a gallery for antiquities which was reopened to the public in 1958. Today the palace belongs to the state; three of its wings are open to visitors, and the fourth is still occupied by the royal family.

kept alive as a fruitful bait for tourists; Kronborg is the "Hamlet castle".

In Sweden at this time most of the fortress-type castles with four corner towers were converted into more habitable houses, or new buildings were put up on the old principle. The most famous of these are Gripsholm – of interest, at least in Europe, because of the charming tale by Kurt Tucholsky – Vadstena and Uppsala, in whose throne room Queen Christina announced her abdication in 1654.

The character of Scandinavian art was predominantly courtly and since Protestantism considerably restricted the building of churches, architecture's most important assignment was the construction of châteaux and palaces. Around Copenhagen there arose the royal palaces of Frederiksborg, Rosenborg and Charlottenborg. Amalienborg, bought by the king after his other residence had burned down, represents a unique form of urban planning.

The North German architect, Nicodemus Tessin, built a summer residence for the royal family of Sweden on the island of Drottningholm. His son had begun to convert Stockholm castle, which was no longer adequate for courtly display, when a fire wrought such destruction that a complete rebuilding became necessary.

Thus at a time when Swedish power had already passed its peak, Stockholm acquired a great Baroque residence in no way inferior to the contemporary palace in Berlin whose architect was Andreas Schlüter, or that in Vienna for which Fischer von Erlach was responsible. In 1763 the Park at Drottningholm was further graced with a charming Rococo pavilion, the "China Palace", yet only twenty years later the palace at Gripsholm was given a theatre complying with all the rules of Classicism; it still has all the original theatrical machinery.

Except for the sober royal residence in Oslo, built during the nineteenth century, Norway possesses no great houses, the Renaissance château built in 1655 and 1656 for the Chancellor, Ore Bjelke, on his estate at Östraat near Trondheim having been destroyed by fire in 1916. But

the ancient coronation city of Trondheim contains the delightful Stiftsgård – an old eighteenth century town house which shows the traditional use of wood in Norwegian building. It is the royal residence in Trondheim.

Amalienborg, Copenhagen. Amalienborg is not a palace in the usual sense of the word, but consists of several separate parts and is significant particularly in the field of town planning. In place of the old residence, four completely identical palaces were built in the district of Frederikstaden for occupation by the four leading noble families of Denmark. They stand at regular intervals around an open octagonal space. Soon after they had been completed, the palace of Christiansborg was burned down in 1794 and, in exchange for it the king bought the whole complex.

Today the royal family lives in the former palace of the Brockdorff family.

Stiftsgård, Trondheim. At the center of the picturesque town of Trondheim lies Stiftsgård, built in 1770 as a residence for the royal family; its façade, painted a deep yellow, conceals a genuine palace with outstanding Rococo decorations. The interior of this, the largest wooden structure in Scandinavia, still serves as a royal residence and is not open to the public.

AUSTRIA

From the time of the late Middle Ages Austria had always formed the basis of the power of the House of Habsburg; during the sixteenth century she became the linchpin of a constantly changing federation of states under the rule of the Habsburgs, whose power as emperors at times extended as far as Spain and the latter's colonies in South America. But Austria was also for a long time seriously threatened by the Turks who had occupied the Balkans and large areas of Hungary.

Thus, in the secular field of architecture, the influence of Renaissance art from nearby Italy was virtually confined to the interior arrangements of castles and strongholds, and could only find unrestricted application in a few places in the far west of the country, where great houses were built such as those at Salzburg and Ambras.

Aside from the architecture promoted by the imperial court, Baroque château building was to find important patrons among the Austrian aristocracy. But it did not start to flourish until after 1683, when the allied Austrian and Polish armies, led by the young prince, Eugene of Savoy, and John Sobieski vanquished the Turks outside Vienna and later drove them out of the areas they had occupied in Hungary, which thus came under Habsburg rule.

Schloss Ambras. The Archduke Ferdinand II presented the castle of Ambras to his wife, Philippine Welser, and in 1564 began to convert the building.

The pièce de résistance of his modernization was the Spanish Saloon, whose decorations derive from Dutch artists.

The master of the house possessed an exceptionally fine collection of weapons and himself owned twenty-five suits of armor. To house these, five armories had to be erected. A few years ago a large part of this collection, including the late Gothic armors for the joust from the Emperor Maximilian I's tiltyard, was returned to Ambras from Vienna.

Schloss Mirabell, Salzburg

The two largest and most uniformly planned great houses in the country, the imperial residence at Schönbrunn and Prince Eugene's Belvedere, arose in Vienna. Their creators were the most outstanding architects of Austrian Baroque; Johann Fischer von Erlach and the somewhat younger Lukas von Hildebrandt, who assimilated the Baroque forms imported from Italy, and turned them into an independent and fertile idiom. Characteristic of these houses is the monumentality of the exterior and the state rooms as compared with the intimacy of the private apartments.

Had the major part of the contents of the

Schloss Mirabell, Salzburg. Nothing survives of Schloss Altenau, built by the archbishop of Salzburg, Wolf Dietrich von Reitenau, for the beautiful Salome Alt, but an engraving by M. Merian. But the people of Salzburg maintain that the female figure on the edge of the fountain in the garden of Mirabell is a portrait of its owner.

After 1721 the castle had to make way for a new building by Lukas von Hildebrandt. This was destroyed by fire, however, in 1818, and only the magnificent Baroque staircase well, with Georg R. Donner's putti, and the Marble Saloon remained; both were incorporated into the next building.

Schloss Schönbrunn, Vienna. Besides the imperial palace in the center of the city, Schönbrunn was the seat of the Habsburg monarchs for over two hundred years. Between 1695 and 1713, Johann Bernhard Fischer von Erlach replaced the royal hunting lodge which had been destroyed by the Turks with a large château complex. Under the rule of the Empress Maria Theresa this received additions in the form of other buildings in the park. The Rococo interior decorations are a good deal more lively than the façades of the rambling building whose profile was formerly lent interest by three large cupolas. Imperial palace architecture inspired much of the château building in Austria, Czechoslovakia and Hungary, widespread use also being made of mellow "Schönbrunn yellow". Between 1746 and 1780, Maria Theresa used to spend the summer here with her family, and it was here, too, that Charles I signed his deed of abdication in 1918, thus putting an end to the Habsburg monarchy.

The imperial carriage standing at the west angle of the palace indicates the carriage collection where all the many varieties of splendid court coaches and equipages are on view. The palace contains 1,441 rooms, of which forty-five are open to the public.

Schloss Belvedere, Vienna (p. 114). Prince Eugene's main residence consists of two buildings, the Upper and the Lower Belvedere, with a garden between them. The more extra-

Belvedere not been so lightly squandered by Prince Eugene's heiress, the house could have given us a better and more comprehensive idea than it does now of the man who, in his own day, was looked on as the "secret emperor", and who succeeded in realizing in astonishing fashion the Baroque passion for universality. When he arrived from France to serve the Emperor Leopold he was poor; at his death he was a multi-millionaire. While he was a general he did not forget the sciences and encouraged plans to set up an academy of sciences and also medical institutes in Vienna; he conducted philos-

ophical discussions with Leibniz, Montesquieu and Rousseau; and in the Belvedere he accumulated rich art collections and a vast library. In the ménagerie there he observed and reared lions, monkeys and exotic birds.

Fischer von Erlach and Lukas von Hildebrandt also worked on Vienna's finest palaces of the aristocracy, such as the Palais Trautson and the Palais Daun-Kinski. By their example and the commissions they undertook outside Vienna they materially determined the course taken by Baroque art in Austria.

vagant Upper Belvedere formed the setting for state occasions; but even the domestic building, the Lower Belvedere, was seldom occupied by its military owner. The sprawling building was completed in 1722. Compared with the severe colonnade of the main façade, the garden side of the house is informal. Under Lukas von Hildebrandt's general supervision, Italian painters and plasterers created interiors of intense beauty. After the owner's death the house passed to the Habsburgs. Belvedere is still used for important state events, and in 1955 the treaty was signed there which restored sovereignty to Austria.

CZECHOSLOVAKIA

During the Middle Ages and under Přemyslid rule Prague was already the focal point of the country; and when the Emperor Charles IV moved his residence to the city, it became one of the cultural and economic centers of the Holy Roman Empire.

One of the two fortified houses there, Prague Castle on the Hradčany, became a splendid royal palace with alternating Romanesque and Gothic buildings. King Vladislav commissioned the architect Benedikt Rejt to build the great Vladislav Hall, in place of Charles IV's palace. The new building possessed not only perfect late Gothic elements, such as rib vaulting, but also early Renaissance forms, thus marking the transition from one style to the other, which coincided with the transition from castle to château architecture.

In Czechoslovakia we find both the usual conversions of existing strongholds and,

Vladislav Hall on the Hradčany, Prague. This banqueting house, more than 180 feet long, was built between 1487 and 1500 by Benedikt Rejt. It combines late Gothic and Renaissance forms. The great hall was even big enough for equestrian sports; subsequently it was used as a throne room, and for royal banquets until 1836. In 1920 the first President of the Republic was ceremonially elected here, and in 1948 the people's democratic constitution was proclaimed.

Belvedere Palace, Prague
Valdštejn Palace, Prague

Belvedere Palace, Prague. Queen Anne's pleasure palace, begun in 1536 by Italian builders, a single block surrounded by arcades, was completed in 1563 by Hans Tirol and Bonifaz Wohlmut who added a second floor containing a ballroom. Rudolph II's court astronomer, Tycho Brahe, worked there; and because of this the building became known as the "mathematical house". During the Thirty Years' War the Swedes not only plundered Rudolph II's art treasures but also the palace furnishings. The pleasure palace for a long time served as a military laboratory until it was restored in 1846 and the upper floor decorated with historical paintings. Since its recent renovation in 1952 the Belvedere has housed works of art. The "singing fountain" in front of the palace is an attraction for tourists.

Valdštejn Palace, Prague. In the Prague Malá Strana (Little Quarter) Duke Albrecht von Wallenstein – known in Czech as Valdštejn – with total disregard for existing streets, houses or city walls, built what was by Prague standards a large early Baroque palace. Around it, in the vineyards below the castle, one palace after another arose. While Valdštejn Palace was being built, the Italian Pieroni erected the Sala Terrena between 1623 and 1627. This banqueting hall was open on the garden side and was richly decorated with paintings and sculptural ornamentation. Today this splendid building serves for festival concerts.

very early, the building of genuine châteaux, executed by Italian masters or under Italian influence. A good example of the latter is Nelahozeves, with rusticated masonry and arcades on the courtyard façade. Under Ferdinand I, Italian architects built the pleasure château, also called the Belvedere, for Queen Anne in the newly laid out royal gardens on the Hradčany. This was the purest early Renaissance building north of the Alps. The Emperor's son, Archduke Ferdinand of Tyrol, had his own ideas incorporated into the Hvězda hunting lodge near Prague; he introduced a somewhat playful variant of the ideal Renaissance ground plan by giving it the form of a six-pointed star.

Schwarzenberg Palace in the Castle Square shows a new and decorative use of an essential element of Italian Renaissance art in its eye-catching walls with their painted faceted rustication. This form of

Hvězda Hunting Lodge, near Prague. In the midst of woodland scenery Archduke Ferdinand built his hunting lodge. The star-shaped building contains six rhomboid rooms in one of which is the staircase. Originally the central section was given emphasis by a cupola, and the acute angles of the building were adorned with small turrets. The ornate stucco decoration has survived, but only faint traces of the painting remain.

façade ornamentation soon became a general favorite both in domestic and civic building, for châteaux, town halls and merchants' houses.

The second Defenestration of Prague, when the imperial governor was thrown from a window of Prague Castle onto a manure heap, unleashed the Thirty Years' War during which Bohemia's rebellious Protestant nobility were defeated by the imperial troops at the Battle of the White Hill in 1620 and were driven out of the country. Their place was taken by alien Catholic aristocrats. The victorious imperial general, Albrecht von Wallenstein, introduced Baroque architecture into Bohemia with his grandiose palace building in Prague. The buildings he commissioned, such as the Sala Terrena, a garden loggia on the Roman pattern erected in the garden of Valdštejn Palace in Prague, were of Italian inspiration.

Kačina Castle, near Prague. Between 1802 and 1822, Count Jan Chotek built a château at the edge of a great forest. In its ground plan it conformed to the horseshoe-shaped Baroque style, but its architectural forms were purely Classical. The low, wide central block is given importance by a heavy, projecting portico. The beautiful Empire furnishings were destroyed in 1945. Since 1950 the building has been used as an agricultural museum.

Česky Krumlov Castle

Česky Krumlov Castle. The medieval castle underwent a thoroughgoing conversion to late Gothic during the sixteenth century, and gradually the complex spread over the entire hillside. The Numismatics Room, the Winter Riding School and the George Chapel were erected in Baroque style. Prince Schwarzenberg who owned Česky Krumlov after 1719, commissioned Josef Lederer in 1748 to decorate the Masque Room – which then, as now, served as a theatre – with gay and brilliantly colored frescos. There figures from Italian comedy gesticulate before the grand occupants of the boxes and the admiring peasants in the auditorium below. A theatre was built, in addition to the Masque Room, in 1766. The castle contains a fine collection of costumes as well as a picture gallery, a display of arts and crafts, and the Numismatics Room.

Hluboká Castle. This château in southern Bohemia occupies the site of a former royal castle of the thirteenth century which was modernized in the sixteenth century. Nothing remains either of this or of the later Baroque conversion carried out by the Schwarzenberg princes. Between 1841 and 1871 the entire building, both within and without, was transformed into English Gothic, so that its profile almost recalls Windsor Castle. The rooms were liberally decorated with trophies of the chase, weapons and examples of the minor arts, while an excellent picture gallery was set up in the riding school and the orangery.

The alien aristocracy sought to demonstrate their own and Habsburg power by the erection of buildings. Thus during the seventeenth century and at the beginning of the eighteenth we find all types of the Baroque palace, in which Viennese prototypes tend to predominate. For the nobility Viennese masters such as Fischer von Erlach designed palaces in Prague which, however, did not exclude the Bohemian love of plastic ornamentation.

The principal master of Prague Baroque was Kilian Ignaz Dientzenhofer upon whose design Kinsky Palace in the Old Town Square is based.

Outside the capital the former fortified structures were again modernized and added to, thus meeting new requirements. But eventually Ferdinand III ordered that the fortifications should be abandoned or destroyed. During the second half of the eighteenth century the foreign aristocracy began to return to the court in Vienna, and consequently fewer Baroque châteaux were built. The turn of the century saw the building of a few Classicist houses, such as Kačina, noteworthy chiefly on account of their fine Empire furnishings. After this, eclecticism made its appearance in what is now Czechoslovakia, and romantically-minded owners transformed Baroque houses into pseudo-medieval strongholds.

SOVIET UNION

Palace of Facets, The Kremlin, Moscow

During the sixteenth century Russia was consolidating her unity as a state under the rule of the Grand Dukes of Moscow and remained relatively unaffected by the cultural and political changes that were taking place in Europe. It is therefore surprising to note that when, at the beginning of the century, the Moscow Kremlin was being converted into a residence fit for the Grand Dukes – the new Tsars of Russia – not only native architects but also Italian artists were

Palace of Facets, The Kremlin, Moscow. The palace, erected between 1487 and 1508 by the Italians Ruffo and Solari, owes its name to the principal ornamentation of its façade, the faceted rustication, that is, diamond-shaped work. The rather large windows, surrounded by heavy stone, were not an altogether fortunate seventeenth century innovation.

In the throne room, where the massive vaults rest upon a single pier at the center, earlier frescos which had been destroyed were replaced by wall paintings done in a style in keeping with the room's former appearance.

Peterhof, near Leningrad. The Frenchman Le Blond was responsible for the designs of the palace and the first buildings to go up in the park. Of the latter "Mon Plaisir" is of particular interest in that it was the Tsar's memento of his stay in Holland. In the low summer pavilion with its Dutch decorations Peter I kept his first paintings by European masters. The principal building was enlarged and altered by Rastrelli after the Tsar's death and that of Le Blond. Rastrelli was also responsible for the pavilions on either side.

The most impressive of all the hydraulic devices and trick fountains in the park is the gilded Samson Fountain in front of the main

building which it often conceals with the spray from its sixty-foot jet. Peterhof was the favorite residence of most of the Tsars and until 1918 was the background to all aspects of court life, especially under the Empresses Elizabeth and Catherine II – aspects which included unbridled indulgence in pleasure as well as palace intrigues. In 1942 park and palace

Winter Palace, Leningrad

*were laid waste and pillaged by Hitler's troops.
But the damage has long since been made good;
and as the palace complex can be quickly
reached by hydrofoil from Leningrad, it is a
great attraction to visitors from all parts of
the Soviet Union and other countries.*

*Winter Palace, Leningrad. The present Winter
Palace building is the fifth to have gone up on
this site. Peter I's modest edifice was followed
by ever larger ones, the last being Rastrelli's
huge quadrangle which he built for Elizabeth in
1759. Little survives of Rastrelli's interior
after the fire of 1837 except for the magnificent
Ambassadors' Staircase. The present interior
derives mostly from the nineteenth century. In
spite of the great array of finery, it is vastly
inferior to the valuable works of art which it
has housed since 1922. The Hermitage collections comprising over two million works of art,
many of them world-famous, are contained in
the palace's 1,050 rooms; and should the visitor
wish to see every work on exhibition, he must
walk over thirteen miles, through 330 rooms.*

*The small original Hermitage building is con-
nected with the Winter Palace; it was commissioned by Catherine II and built by Leo
von Klenze to house her rapidly increasing
collection of art treasures. It was in the Winter
Palace that the Kerensky government capitulated
in 1917. Even before the Second World War
was over, a start had been made on repairing
the severe damage caused to the palace by gunfire
during the siege of Leningrad.*

Tsars' Palace, Pushkin
Ostankino Palace, near Moscow

Tsars' Palace, Pushkin. What was formerly known as Tsarskoye Selo, or "Tsars' village", was renamed Pushkin in 1937 after the famous writer who grew up there. The luxury-loving Empress Elizabeth, Catherine I's daughter, commissioned Rastrelli to transform her mother's modest summer residence into a gigantic palace with a richly gilded façade. To the more sober mind of Catherine II this was extravagant ostentation and she had it removed.

The principal palace, which is almost a thousand feet in width, was named after her; she had the left wing reconstructed by Charles Cameron, the Scottish architect, and her private rooms redecorated in Classical style incorporating, however, the Russian love of costly materials such as choice woods, alabaster, agate, silk brocades and amber.

The complete wall covering of amber which had been bought from King Frederick William I of Prussia and incorporated in the famous "Amber Room" was, however, removed during the German occupation and has not yet been located.

The palace and grounds formed part of the front line during the Second World War and were almost wholly destroyed. Since then all the buildings have been restored and work on the interior is proceeding. Scattered about the park are a number of small buildings, pavilions and luxuriously equipped bath houses, such as the Upper Bath House with its hot and cold baths. Many of these miniature buildings are built in exotic styles such as Chinese or Turkish.

Ostankino Palace, near Moscow. The estate of Ostankino came into the possession of Count Sheremetev in 1743. He was famed for encouraging the creative talents of his many serfs. Between 1792 and 1797 his own architects built the Classicist palace from a design by Quarenghi. It contains a picture gallery with valuable West European works and also a theatre which, in the Count's day, was renowned for having the best company of actor serfs in Russia. During the Napoleonic campaign French troops were quartered in Ostankino which was indifferently restored after their departure. But it has since been thoroughly renovated and is now open to visitors.

engaged upon the work. Almost contemporaneous with the famous Kremlin churches is the Palace of Facets built under the direction of the Italians, Marco Ruffo and Pietro Solari; it was the first building in Russia to which details in the style of the European Renaissance were applied. Terem Palace in the Kremlin, built a hundred years later, testifies to the skill of its Russian architects who were also responsible for the palaces commissioned by the nobility in the town of Moscow.

A tremendous impetus was given to Russian, and more especially to château architecture, by the activities of Peter I. The foundation of the new capital at St. Petersburg necessitated the building of ostentatious palaces which, thanks to the Tsar's veneration for all that was latest in Western European thought, incorporated in their plans the most advanced art forms. Foreign artists were summoned to St. Petersburg, the most important being the Italians Trezzini, Chiaveri and Rinaldi, and the Frenchmen Le Blond – who also drew up a plan for the layout of the city of St. Petersburg – and Vallin de la Mothe; there was also the German architect Andreas Schlüter. Collaborating with these artists were the Russians Semtsov and Rastrelli, of whom the latter was subsequently to become pre-eminent. The first palaces were built on the banks of the Neva. As early as 1704 Peter the Great had himself selected the site for Peterhof on Kronstadt Bay. From the beginning the intention was to make Peterhof one of the largest and most beautiful combinations of park and palace in the world. The plan included buildings scattered about the park, water pavilions

and sculptures. Its apotheosis was the palace itself, built on a rise and connected with the sea by a cascade and a canal.

Peterhof is clearly distinguished by the characteristics of Russian palace architecture – the generous use of space, together with a love of the monumental which blends strangely with a predilection for detail.

The combination of these two aspects is in even greater evidence in the palace ensemble at Pushkino, the former Tsarskoye Selo. This began as a simple palace for the Tsarina Catherine I; under Elizabeth it was transformed into a vast complex executed by the master of Russian Baroque, Rastrelli, while Catherine II, summoning the Scottish architect, Charles Cameron, to St. Petersburg for the purpose, added Classicist pavilions and colonnades so that eventually the complex emulated, though it could not outdo, the French standard set by Versailles.

In the center of the city, too, the vast rectangular Winter Palace, designed by Rastrelli, arose on the banks of the Neva. After its storming in the October Revolution it became known throughout the world as a symbol of Tsardom, although since 1905 Nicholas II, the last of the Tsars, had lived only at Tsarskoye Selo.

It was not only the Tsars who built palaces. After Peter III had freed the aristocracy from their obligatory service to the state, they were able to return to their estates and possessions, and this resulted in the building of country houses and noble palaces. The work was carried out, sometimes by known masters, but often by builders who were serfs, as in the case of Ostankino Palace near Moscow.

Catherine II was largely responsible for having encouraged Classicism at an early date, and this style is represented both in the building done at the castle at Pavlovsk and in many palaces built by the nobility, as well as in public edifices in Leningrad and Moscow.

One of these palaces, Smolny, founded by Catherine II as a school "for young ladies", has a façade designed by Quarenghi in 1808. It became the headquarters of the Petersburg Soviet, and it was from there that Lenin directed the Revolution in 1917, whose victory, almost at a blow, deprived the palaces and great houses throughout the land of their exclusivity. Instead, either then or later, they were put to uses which could be of service to all the people.

Nothing is left of the palaces of the Hungarian kings except contemporary descriptions and architectural fragments which confirm the veracity of those sources. Our picture of the great royal palaces of the fourteenth and early fifteenth centuries has been further added to by the excavations made at Visegrád, Buda and Esztergom.

There were important artistic achievements during the reign of King Matthias Corvinus who also encouraged the dissemination of Renaissance culture from Italy, greatly to the benefit of château architecture. However this promising beginning was brought to an abrupt close by the defeat at Mohács. Hungarian territory came under three spheres of influence: the largest, central area was ruled by the Turks; the north-west was occupied by the Austrian Habsburgs; and Transylvania was ruled by a *voivode* (leader) who for a long time remained a vassal of the Turks.

Renaissance principles continued to op-

Ráckeve Palace. In *1760* Prince Eugene of Savoy commissioned the architect Lukas von Hildebrandt to build a palace on his estate at Ráckeve. On a small island in the Danube, Hildebrandt built what was the first secular Baroque building in Hungary. It has often been regarded as an experimental model for Schloss Belvedere which he began ten years later in Vienna. The building had many owners and underwent many changes. For instance the

original cupola resembling that of a Chinese pagoda has not survived.

For this reason the historical interest of the building was only recognized about ten years ago when reconstruction was begun. It is still proceeding. The house contains the Arpad Museum.

Episcopal Palace, Vezprém. In *1765* the architect Jakob Fellner built this late Ba-

roque episcopal palace on the site of a medieval royal palace. Transverse wings still suggest a Baroque style cour d'honneur, *but this is only just large enough to allow some space between the projecting, covered approach and the street.*

The sparse ornamentation combines Rococo elements with features of the sober German Zopfstil. *The building is still used for its original ecclesiastical purpose.*

erate in architecture until the seventeenth century in Transylvania and in the Habsburg area. Italian influence prevailed and it was mainly Italian architects who were responsible for erecting houses for the Hungarian aristocracy. One that is worthy of mention is Nagybiccse, a sixteenth century quadrangular structure with four round, squat corner towers and a tall gatehouse tower.

By the seventeenth century there was in the Habsburg area a Baroque movement which was closely connected with the Counter-Reformation. Protestantism had gained a considerable footing in Hungary and every effort was made to suppress it. Not only were large Baroque churches built, in order to impress the people, but also splendid episcopal palaces, as at Vezprém.

The Austrian rulers themselves, however, did little building in Hungary. Buda Castle was rebuilt at this time, but nothing of it has survived.

After the victory of the Austrian army which, with the help of Polish forces, defeated the Turks outside Vienna and subsequently drove them out of Hungary, the Peace of Karlowitz brought nearly the whole of that country under the do-

minion of Austria. In 1702 Prince Eugene commissioned his Viennese architect, Lukas von Hildebrandt, to build him a mansion at Ráckeve. Round about the middle of the eighteenth century the powerful Hungarian nobility also began ostentatious building – for instance, the palaces of Grassalkovich, Gödöllö and Esterházy, the latter at Fertöd. They show clear indications of French influence while their detail comprises the Rococo elements of the time.

The more progressive among the Hungarian nobility, however, did not come to terms with the Habsburgs but took part in the national movement of liberation against that monarchy. These aristocrats were less concerned with parading their own wealth than with patriotic interests such as education or national artistic endeavor, so that instead of great houses there arose museums, theatres and other civic buildings.

Esterház y Palace, Fertöd. Around the hunting lodge built in 1721 the largest château in Hungary arose between 1764 and 1766.

It was commissioned by the powerful Prince Nicholas Esterház y, known as "the lover of splendor", who himself made alterations to the designs prepared by Melchior Hefele. The three-story main block is unusual in that it curves around three sides of the courtyard which is then completely enclosed by single-story wings. Its extensive grounds containing pavilions, as well as its interior, in particular the Chinese and Porcelain Rooms, the armory, the picture gallery and the puppet theatre, set the standard for many lesser houses in Hungary. The opera house, which has since been demolished, was the scene of brilliant operas and concerts since Joseph Haydn was in the service of the Prince of Esterház y between 1760 and 1790.

Most of the buildings attached to the estate are now occupied by an agricultural research station. Because of its wealth of musical associations, festival concerts regularly take place in this great house.

ROMANIA

The keynote of the country's history from the fourteenth century up till the Crimean War in 1856 was the struggle against the Turks. In the Middle Ages three countries existed on what is now Romanian territory – Walachia, Moldavia and Transylvania, though by the eleventh century the latter had become part of Hungary. After the Turkish victory at Mohács, Transylvania became subject to the Turks, but in the two other territories it was only after prolonged resistance that the chief boyars, or high nobility, surrendered to Turkish domination to preserve their own power. Thus the aristocracy remained a ruling caste on sufferance under the Ottoman Empire, sometimes siding with the Turks against their own people, sometimes with the people against the oppressor. Such conditions were, of course, hardly calculated to encourage the building of fine houses.

It was in the sixteenth century that the

Magna Curia Castle, Deva. The Transylvanian prince Gabriel Bethlen who for many years headed his country's resistance against Turkish rule, had the twelfth-century castle converted into a château in 1612. It shows the transition, typical of the time, from late Renaissance forms to Baroque. It now serves as the central museum for the Hunedoara-Deva region.

Mogoșoaia Palace, near Bucharest. Prince Constantin Brîncoveanu's residence was completed in 1702. This building has all the special characteristics of the style which evolved during Brîncoveanu's thirty years' reign, namely Byzantine elements combined with Venetian features, such as open loggias. The palace was looted after the prince's death, and fell into decay. It was restored in 1860 and since 1957 has been used to house the collections of feudal art from the Museum of Art of the Romanian Republic. The exhibits are mainly concerned with the art and culture of Brîncoveanu's time.

Peleș Castle, Sinaia. In the foothills of the Bucegi Mountains, Prince Charles of Hohenzollern built a summer residence whose exterior resembled those pseudo-medieval strongholds, complete with turrets and panel work, that were so popular in Germany towards the end of the nineteenth century. Within, however, there is an inconsequent medley of Italian, German, and English neo-Renaissance elements, combined with Baroque, Rococo and Spanish-Saracenic forms. During the sixty years that Peleș served as a summer residence there was in its vicinity a mushroom growth of villas, palaces and luxury hotels for rich Romanians. Sinaia grew to be one of the most important and beautiful health resorts. Since the war Peleș Castle has served a new purpose as a museum.

first Renaissance châteaux were built in
Transylvania – a territory that only became
part of Romania in 1918 – at Vinţul
de Jos, on the banks of the Criş and
in Bonţida.

The Bruckenthal Palace at Sibiu and the
castle of Magna Curia built at Deva
below the citadel for the Transylvanian
prince Bethlen, who led a rising to lib-
erate the country, are fine examples of
Romanian Baroque.

Under Constantin Brîncoveanu, the ruler
of Walachia, who entered into a secret
alliance with Peter I of Russia against the
Turks, there arose the castles of Potlogi,
Mogoşoaia and Brîncoveni. Mogoşoaia,
the residence outside the gates of Bucharest is, for central Europe, a comparatively
small and unpretentious structure;
despite certain affinities to Venetian
architecture, it has a charm that is all
its own and which is due, perhaps, to its
setting in a wild landscape and to its
small artificial lake. Towards the end of
the nineteenth century, Charles von Hohen-
zollern-Sigmaringen, who in 1866 became
prince and in 1881 king of Romania,
built a summer residence at Sinaia – Peleş
Castle. Here, as elsewhere in Europe,
Germany's export of royalty brought into
being a fairy tale castle, for Peleş
derives from the memory of German
strongholds.